It's Your Move

How to Motivate Yourself and Your Family

It's Your Move

How to Motivate Yourself and Your Family

John W. Drakeford

Fleming H. Revell Company
Old Tappan, New Jersey

Library of Congress Cataloging in Publication Data

Drakeford, John W.
  It's your move.

  1. Success.   2. Christian life—Baptist authors.
I. Title.
BJ1611.2.D73   1985   158′.1   85-2131
ISBN 0-8007-1425-3

To the presidents, faculty, and students of Southwestern Baptist Theological Seminary, that band of comrades in the Christian pilgrimage who for thirty years have nurtured, challenged and caused me to remember, "It's Your Move."

Contents

Preface

My aim in this book is to persuade my reader that whatever his circumstances and those of his family, they do not have to stay the way they are. It is possible to take a DECISIVE MOTIVATIONAL ACTION.

The ACTION IMPERATIVE, in many ways so obvious, and the basis of the best in our society, is so frequently overlooked that we need to be recalled to this fundamental concept.

In one of those situations which infrequently arise, my wife and I found ourselves in London for a week and decided to take advantage of a guided walking tour of sites associated with the writings of Charles Dickens. At the spot where the Saracen's Head Inn had once stood, our guide reminded us that this was the spot where Nicholas Nickleby had first met Wackford Squeers and began his career as a teacher in Squeers' notorious school in Yorkshire.

The incident sent me to rereading the book, *Nicholas Nickleby,* and discovering that many Dickens scholars believe a large portion of the novel is autobiographical and thus gives insights into the functioning of his remarkable personality.

Nicholas Nickleby is a book about a family, a pitiable little family, consisting of Nicholas 19, Kate 17, and Mrs. Nickleby. The late Mr. Nickleby, at his wife's urgings, had invested all his assets and, with the collapse of the stock market, lost every penny. In reaction to this experience Mr. Nickleby took to his bed, deteriorated rapidly into irrationality, and died, leaving his family in a poverty-stricken condition.

Mr. Nickleby's brother Ralph, who resided in London, had been successful in the business world, and the impoverished little family set out for that city, to seek the help of their prosperous relative. Unfortunately Ralph turned out to be a tight-fisted misanthrope whose main objective appeared to be to get his brother's family off his hands as quickly as he could.

Ralph Nickleby's attitude toward the bonds of family life is seen when Mrs. Nickleby informed him that his brother died of a broken heart. Ralph responded, "Pooh! There's no such thing. I can understand a man's dying of a broken neck, or suffering from a broken arm, or a broken head ... but a broken heart!—nonsense, it's the cant of the day. If a man can't pay his debts, he dies of a broken heart, and his widow's a martyr."[1]

This introduction of the Nickleby family sets the theme for the total novel, which is built around their fortunes as a family. They make a rather pathetic group: the innocent, seventeen-year-old Kate bereft of any marketable skills; Mrs. Nickleby, a dithering and ineffective head of the group; and Nicholas, imaginative but inexperienced and gullible, moving like a lamb in the midst of a pack of marauding wolves. The prospects for this family do not look good.

When Nicholas accepted the position of teacher in the notorious school of Wackford Squeers, he was immediately confronted with another aspect of the family concept, and saw firsthand a parody of the intentional family. In London, while recruiting new students, Squeers was threatening a small boy who dissolved into tears. As he suddenly espied the parent of a prospective student approaching, Squeers's whole demeanor changed and he commenced a mealy-mouthed harangue of the boy, ". . . you will have a father in me and a mother in Mrs. Squeers."[2]

Later he again took up the theme with Nicholas as he held forth on the alleged virtues of his wife in relation to the students. "She is more than a mother to them; ten times more. She does things for them boys, Nickleby, that I don't believe half the mothers going, would do for their own sons."[3] Things like "treacling" them—pushing an enormous wooden spoon of brimstone and treacle into their mouths and compelling them to devour the loathsome mess in one gulp—and wiping her treacly hands on one curly headed boy's hair.

All of this pious cant about the school being a family was mouthed by Squeers while he was running a boarding school which was in reality more like a prison camp than a family.

Yet through it all, the pitiable Nickleby family proved to be a bulwark against the vicissitudes of their stormy surroundings. Amid all the brutality and venality associated with nineteenth-century London life the family continued on as the provider of love, the one factor more important than the struggle for economic survival and the one indispensable element in a family experience.

Dickens was more than a writer. He was a social crusader and focused the reader's attention on the social evils of his day. He could have been satisfied to write and live on his considerable earnings from his craft, but he chose to write with a purpose. One of Dickens's friends once described the reaction of the author to news of people who had been unfairly treated, "He used to blaze with indignation when he heard of any wrong or injustice."

The character Nickleby did not just blaze. Living as a

poorly paid teacher in the boarding school of the tyrannical Squeers, Nicholas was horrified by what he saw. But he was determined to be tactful and repress his reactions to Squeers's sadistic behavior.

Then came the moment when Squeers was about to brutally flog the unfortunate boy named Smike. Nicholas rushed to Squeers and intervened, crying out in indignation, "I will not stand by and see it done."

Whether the story was autobiographical or not, this phrase became the keynote of Dickens's writing—he was a man of action. As a result of Dickens's actions many of the laws and social practices of the England of his day were radically changed.

Although not in any way even approaching Dickens as a writer, I have a similar objective. I am aiming to motivate an action in the reader's life. However, I am not focusing on the institutions of society, but on the individual himself and his immediate family.

Central to my objective is the concept of the Decisive Motivational Action, which I state in summary form in each chapter. Each word in these statements is significant, but it is the Action Premise that is vital.

In recent years a whole new breed of individuals, generally referred to as activists, has come to the fore. They are generally people who are upset by some aspect of society around them and are determined to change things.

Activists are not satisfied to wait for an evolutionary development of society but insist that something must be done, and done immediately. Because activists are sometimes vociferous in their condemnation of the prevailing system and may go so far as to advocate its destruction, the term *activist* has developed some undesirable connotations. It is very important that there be no confusion, that the reader get the idea that I am on the side of the activist. I am not. What I am advocating is a different type of activity.

Not Activist but Actionist

Because of these associations we are going to make a careful distinction between being an activist and an AC-TIONIST.

Activist	Actionist
Aims to change society.	Works on changing himself and others by example.
Has a critical, negative message of what is wrong.	Is positively aware of opportunities and possibilities.
Will use vigorous force if he thinks it necessary.	Believes in the power of individual persuasion.
Wedded to a political philosophy.	Interested in philosophy of personal fulfillment.
Operates on people's emotions-agitation as a means to stir up.	May make emotional appeals, but is basically seeking to influence the will.

The actionist does not spend his time pointing a finger at society in general or individuals in particular. He doesn't call in strident tones for society to change. He does something himself and seeks primarily to change himself. He may ultimately change society but that is not his fundamental task nor that of this book.

Preface

The Actionist Par Excellence

Our Lord Jesus Christ was an actionist. "I must work the works of him that sent me," He said. When He took a journey, it was said that "he must needs go through Samaria." He lived under a compulsion to act. And in moving toward the climactic deed of His life, "He steadfastly set his face to go to Jerusalem."

This same Actionist called upon His followers to act. The word *go* was constantly on His lips. In the development of the concept of faith in the New Testament, as we will later see, faith gives rise to action. Jesus presented the law of momentum: "For unto every one that hath shall be given, and he shall have abundance; but from him that hath not shall be taken away even that which he hath" (Matthew 25:29). The follower of the lowly Nazarene lives under the imperative of action.

Like the book *Nicholas Nickleby,* in which there are two major themes, action and family, in this book we will place the emphasis on the action of the individual and that of the family as they constitute themselves into an action unit that undertakes a series of Decisive Motivational Actions.

What are we waiting for?

It's Your Move

HOW TO *MOTIVATE* YOURSELF
AND YOUR FAMILY

1

How to Get You and Your Family off the Mark

The rung of the ladder was never meant to rest upon, but only to hold a man's foot long enough to put the other somewhat higher.

Thomas Huxley

 Ask someone the difference between an American and an Englishman and there is a good chance he will say the Englishman is more conservative, more staid, more stiff upper lip, while the American is more energetic, brash, more of a hustler. If you apply these criteria to riders on an escalator you are wrong, wrong, wrong.

Mount an escalator in an American airport and you'll find people largely ignoring the signs that tell them, "Standers to the right, walkers to the left." They drape themselves in various poses across the moving handrails, stand chatting with friends, gazing out into space as if watching a UFO, and, by and large, looking as if they are taking a leisurely voyage down the river on a Sunday afternoon.

What a contrast in a British subway. The tired commuters who don't feel like walking stand close to the side of the escalator, leaving a clear run for those in a hurry. This happy breed of hustlers go hurrying up or down the escalator and if an unfortunate tourist stands in the way they give him a gentle, "I say, old chap, would you mind moving over?"

The Modern Blitzkrieg

So too with the allegedly phlegmatic Germans. For all who have lamented the rush of an American freeway it might be a good idea to take a trip down a German autobahn. These motorists are in a hurry and even though gasoline is expensive and the Teutonic tendency towards calculation and evaluation must have told them that speed eats up their costly fuel, they nevertheless thunder down the autobahn with no speed limits to impede their progress.

DECISIVE MOTIVATIONAL ACTION #1

Life demands action. If you do not take advantage of the situation, someone else will. MOVE ON OR MOVE OVER. Learn that there is an action answer for every situation in life.

If you are pushing your Volkswagen bus at a mere sixty miles per hour you had better keep to the right. The inner lane is reserved for drivers of the powerful European jobs which may eat up the highway at speeds of one hundred twenty miles per hour.

Supposing you are caught behind a slower vehicle and you decide to pass—no mean feat in an older model VW— and you get into that inside lane. There's a good chance that within moments you'll feel as if you're back in the days of Hitler's blitzkrieg. In daytime, the sound of the horn of a would-be passer will assault your ears, and at night you may imagine you are flying over enemy territory with search-lights stabbing their beams at you, as an impatient motorist flashes his lights in an obvious message of, "get over in the other lane." SLOW TRAFFIC TO THE RIGHT is taken very literally in Germany.

Even though you're on the right track you're still going to be run over if you don't move.

The memory of struggling along the autobahn in a VW, with occasional excursions into the no man's land of the fast lane, still returns at times to haunt me. I wish we could in-still the simple rule, SLOW TRAFFIC TO THE RIGHT, in American motorists' minds. Although technically a rule on U.S. highways, it is more honored in the breach than in the observance. Many a cluttered American highway is that way largely because a few thoughtless drivers wander down the center of the highway, holding up the traffic flow and helping to bring ulcers to many a hurrying driver striving desperately to pass.

MOVE ON OR MOVE OVER—that's the message of life.

Just because you want to dawdle it doesn't mean others are willing to stay at your pace. They are going to move and you are going to be left behind. And what is true of individu-als is equally true of families. A family is a living, vital unit and it must move and adapt itself to the environment sur-rounding it.

Respond to Crisis with Action

What does a patriotic American citizen, a graduate of the Naval Academy and the quintessence of law-abiding respectability, do when he discovers his country is bogged down in a diplomatic dialog with another nation and nothing is being accomplished?

He says by his actions, MOVE ON OR MOVE OVER.

Possibly the most humiliating national experience of the 1970s came when Iranian demonstrators climbed the wall of the American Embassy building in Tehran and took possession of the embassy, holding the staff as hostages for an agonizing 444 days. In the strange way that history has of reversing situations, the '70s also produced evidence that the spirit of adventure characterizing the American dream was still alive and well. Characteristically, in this twentieth century, the leader of an enterprise that would leave an Errol Flynn movie standing still was a crew-cut, business-suited leader of a great computer company, Ross Perot.

The president of Electronic Data Services, Perot had built his highly successful enterprise by moving into international markets. One of these efforts resulted in winning a contract to computerize the social security organization in the Ministry of Health and Welfare of the government of Iran. The enterprise moved along successfully, but meanwhile, political unrest was mounting toward the maelstrom that ultimately deposed the Shah and plunged the country into chaos. It also gave rise to the final indignity of Americans held hostage and the embarrassing debacle of a failed rescue attempt.

In the midst of the mounting chaos two EDS employees, Paul Chiaparone and Bill Gaylord, were jailed on a trumped-up charge and informed that they would remain in prison unless they produced $13 million for bail. The amount was indicative of the intention to keep them in prison. The situation looked grim.

Perot began to use his considerable influence in the highest circles of the American government, but all of the efforts of the U.S. ambassador to Iran were in vain. The Iranians had a word which they constantly used, *fardah,* usually translated "tomorrow." In actual practice it meant, "sometime in the future"; *fardah* seemed to be the irritating attitude of the authorities with regard to the situation.

But Perot, the aggressive Texan, wasn't about to accept this stalemated situation. Realizing his men might rot in jail or be destroyed in the rapidly developing revolution, he decided to do something. He would organize a rescue effort to gain his men's release.

When he shared his plan with a senior executive of the company, the response was, "I think that is the world's worst idea."

Perot replied, "I talked Paul and Bill into going over there, and I'm going to get them out."

For Perot, sentiment was not a mournful emotion but a clarion call for action.

He enlisted the leadership of retired army officer Colonel "Bull" Simon and a team of six men who went into a training program in which they meticulously planned every detail of the rescue effort. So detailed was their preparation that they improvised a setting in which they rehearsed the actual rescue over two hundred times.

The author of the account of the rescue titled *On Eagle's Wings* has written several fiction thrillers, but none of them is more compelling than the story of Colonel Simon and his men leading in the escape of Chiaparone and Gaylord. They outmaneuvered a vengeful magistrate, moved around Tehran in the midst of a revolution, manipulated avaricious Iranians, took a nightmare automobile trip across Iran, evaded would-be captors, talked their way out of interrogations, negotiated their way past trigger-happy revolutionaries at numerous roadblocks and finally crossed the border into Turkey.

Of Perot the writer said, "He responded to crisis with action."

The simple theme of this book you are now reading is:

THERE IS AN ACTION ANSWER TO EVERY
SITUATION IN LIFE.
THE VERY WORST THING YOU CAN DO IS—NOTHING.

In this volume we are going to follow the implications of THE ACTION IMPERATIVE.

A Family Is A Dynamic Interacting Unit

Our journey may turn out to be an adventure in many ways comparable to that of the Iranian rescue group. This team of seven men was in many ways a family, an intentional family, which like many modern-day families was moving in an unsympathetic environment but survived and ultimately triumphed because of its aggressive actions. Like this intentional group, our modern families, beset with challenges on every hand, must commit themselves to a program of action.

Traditionally the family has fulfilled many functions, but five of them stand out:

1. It provided an economic undergirding. Families of yesteryear were a team that worked the farm, milked the cows,

and harvested the crops. Each family member was an important part of the income-producing process.

2. It gave protection to the family members. In the more primitive times the family would band together to face enemies or invaders. The weaker members of the family and the ill were seen to be the responsibility of the total group.

3. It cultivated moral standards. Values were learned in the context of the family and they were seen as playing an important part in preserving its viability. Marriage was highly respected and seen as the vehicle for expressing sexuality and passing on the family heritage.

4. It educated the young. All education commenced within the family and this very naturally included the passing on of great religious truths to the young.

5. It conferred status. People were proud of the family from which they came, and the surrounding society in evaluating an individual said, "He comes from a good family."

The Way It Is Now

These five factors were part of the way a family used to be, but things have changed.

1. The family is no longer an economic asset and children have become a financial liability.

2. Society provides protection and security, and in some instances will not allow a family to build its own defenses.

3. The family, as an educational institution, has been replaced by a state system which may tell parents they cannot educate their children.

4. Great numbers of people no longer hold the old views of the sanctity of marriage, the importance of moral standards or religious teaching. Sexuality may find expression

without benefit of marriage and commitment among many people.

5. For many, the family doesn't confer status anymore. Many belong to a family in which some of the members even have different surnames, and there is little cohesion. It is no matter of pride to them that they are members of this family.

The situation has caused many pessimists to conclude that the family might well have had its day. This attitude is not as new as some would think. Back in 1934 a commission concluded that the original reasons for the family's existence had disappeared and the family itself would shortly vanish. Patricia Harris put it well when she said that when Cain slew Abel, Adam probably turned to Eve and said, "The future of the family is in jeopardy."

The pessimists have overlooked one aspect of family life—its uncommon capacity for adaptation. The family is a remarkably resilient institution, constantly changing and accommodating itself to new sets of circumstances.

The family must of necessity *move*. Consequently it is an appropriate subject for the application of the ACTION IMPERATIVE.

FOR THE PERSON OF FAITH, THE WORD FAMILY
IS NOT SO MUCH A SENTIMENT AS A CLARION
CALL FOR ACTION

Move from Attitude to Action

Attend any sales conference, talk to any high-powered promoter, listen to the testimony of someone highly successful in his field and you are going to hear the expression PMA. The Positive Mental Attitude has been the theme song of the world of the motivator, and it has done yeoman service. But it can be misunderstood.

The trouble with attitudes is that they can be *static*.

The word *attitude* is related to the word *aptitude* and literally means "posture." It was originally used for describing the Greek athlete in a posture of readiness—readiness to respond to the starting signal. But what if the athlete was forever in his posture but never leaped into action? Always on the starting line but never took off down the track?

An Attitude Is A Posture of The Mind

Napoleon Bonaparte used to say that every French soldier had a marshal's baton in his knapsack. I'm equally convinced that a good proportion of the literate public have a book in their heads.

When I'm introduced to any number of people as an author, at least one and generally more than one person says, "We've got something in common. I'm going to write a book."

I respond, "I'd like to read it."

"Oh, I haven't written it yet, but...," he says, tapping his forehead, "I've got it in here. It's just waiting to come out. I'm going to put it down on paper one of these days. When I have time."

I usually murmur something about wishing the would-be writer well. "I hope the book is a best-seller." If I were honest I'd say, "Millions of people have *thought* about writing a book. At the moment, you have an idea, an ephemeral thought, which may come and go; it has no permanence, no certain existence. You don't have a book until you act—until you put it down on paper." From the Positive Mental Attitude you must move on to another stage; there must be *action*.

The Action Premise

The basic premise of this book is action. Not *any* action, but action of a certain type—the Decisive Motivational Action.

The ideal man as seen here is the actionist. A college motto reads, "WHEN YOU WAKE UP, GET UP; WHEN YOU GET UP, DO SOMETHING." This is the life of the actionist. If you believe that the summum bonum of life is to sit in a chair and rock, read no further; this book is not for you. Put it down and retire to your rocking chair.

WHEN YOU WAKE UP, GET UP
WHEN YOU GET UP, DO SOMETHING

But if you are aware that idleness is debilitating and leaves you with a sense of uneasiness, and that there must be more to life than doing nothing, read on. Sample a little of the world of the actionist.

Although, as we will later see, the Christian faith is a process of dynamic action, it is all too easy to give the impression that it consists in negatives—what we don't do.

Majoring on Negatives

I went into the army happily and proudly. World War II days where I lived were devoid of protestors; a warm patriotism coupled with the awareness of significant national threat propelled me into uniform. As a chaplain I was conscious of my spiritual responsibilities and determined to stand by my convictions.

My first test came when the colonel met me at the mess and introduced me to my fellow officers and then, "How about a whiskey?" he asked.

I swallowed and responded, "Thank you, sir, but I don't drink."

As we stood chatting, a major offered me a cigarette. "I appreciate it, but I don't smoke," I said.

About this time a bright-eyed lieutenant came rushing up and said, "Hi. Say, you're new here, aren't you? We're having a dance on Saturday night and need another officer to escort one of our nurses. How about it?"

I smiled weakly. "Sorry, I don't dance."

A sun-tanned captain standing nearby observed all this and at last he spoke: "Chaplain, do you spit?"

All my virtues were negatives. This incident along with others since has compelled me to think of the importance of action in all areas of life, particularly the life of faith.

Mark Twain in his unique way stated the situation, "It is noble to be good, it is nobler to help someone else be good, and easier." We are not going to focus on others, but on ourselves. This is the pathway of the actionist; he is working on himself.

The Christian Actionist

All of this applies particularly to the Christian. Many people have a *faith attitude*. For some this is just a statement: "Of course I am a Christian. I reside in a Christian country and I try to live the Christian life." For others, being a Christian is a much more vital matter involving a definite decision—but a decision that did not lead to any action. Such a faith attitude is deficient in one vital area.

James addresses himself to the faith attitude and says, "What doth it profit, my brethren, though a man say he hath faith, and have not works?" (James 2:14). The faith attitude is not what the Bible calls faith. It is deficient in the area of action. It is but a prelude to faith. To become a balanced, biblical experience it must lead to action.

The Actionist Family

The concept of the family embodies many of the noblest ideals of mankind, and words like *mother, father, children, babies* and *love* evoke some of the noblest emotions. It is relatively easy to pay tribute to these ideals. What cynic would dare raise his voice against them?

But here again, attitude must be transformed into action. Positive sentiment alone will not suffice. The mere passage of time means that a family will pass through several stages of development, and each stage calls for adaptation. I would identify these stages in the following way:

1. Courtship and marriage. A new family unit starts in the most unlikely way in an experience when two people are attracted to each other and elect to marry. It is a time of action as they decide the basis on which they could unite, develop at least some understanding about role expectations as husband and wife and, hopefully, come to understand the family of their intended spouses.

2. Childbearing Years. The arrival of children calls for a series of actions by husband and wife. Hopefully, the husband develops a sense of financial responsibility, gives lead-

ership to the family and assists in the household chores, and follows through with masculine input into the growth and development and spiritual awakening of the children.

For her part, the wife moves through her distinctive act of creativity in pregnancy to the nurturing activities associated with school and church. From night feedings and diapers she goes on to the experiences of PTA and Little League.

But let these parents beware lest they become too immersed in these tasks. The skills they have learned will have to be surrendered. The main task of parents is to prepare their children to get along without them. New and different actions lie ahead.

3. The empty nest. Children are soon gone and the house becomes strangely silent. In the modern family the new period of the "empty nest," like so many others in family life, can present pitfalls or potentialities. If the children have been the major focus of the family there may be problems at this stage. It could be that husband and wife have become a couple of strangers living under the same roof, and they will find themselves with time on their hands.

The appropriate action for a husband and wife is to learn the most effective ways of utilizing the time they have together and when the time comes that they are alone, to do the things they have dreamed about for so long. It might well be that they will discover some wonderful new potentialities in their relationship. But only if they take the appropriate actions.

4. Becoming grandparents. With the departure of children and their marriage and new babies comes the sense of the development of a clan. Grandchildren are so much more enjoyable than children. As one grandparent put it, "It's wonderful to be a grandparent. We take the children, play

with them and enjoy them. Then comes the end of the day, when they are dirty, tired, and cranky and we call their parents and tell them to come and pick up *their* kids."

If freedom from responsibility is the hallmark of being a grandparent, another responsibility is lurking nearby as the grandparents come to terms with caring for their own parents. A measure of the viability of a family is the way in which they accept responsibility for the older family members. One of the saddest verses in all the Bible is, "Cast me not off in the time of old age; forsake me not when my strength faileth" (Psalms 71:9).

So the family continues on, often unaware of the peculiar function it is fulfilling. It was said of the family of Jonathan and Sarah Edwards that its influence was so pervasive that it could well be called the Gulf Stream of American colonial life. Our families have a similar potential, but only if they move from attitude to action, and take the proper actions at the appropriate time in their development.

TO BE GOOD IS NOBLE
TO HELP SOMEONE ELSE BE GOOD IS BETTER
AND EASIER

2
No-Go,
Slow-Go or Go-Go?

It is essential that the action we are speaking of here be seen as a motivational action. As we undertake these actions they lead on to other important experiences. Action that is an end in itself is of no real value. The word *motivate* relates to the goad, the spur that pushes an individual from one level to another.

I am thinking of my childhood days when we managed through the winter with the scant warmth of a simple wood or coal fire. When we retired to bed in the evening we kept warm with extra clothing, piling up blankets and covers and putting our feet on bricks, heated for the purpose, and wrapped in newspaper. Body warmth fended off the cold of the winter's night, but rising in the morning was a test of character.

We knew nothing of the luxury of carpets. Our floors were covered with linoleum kept shining bright with frequent applications of polish by my industrious mother. Unfortunately, linoleum has an affinity for coolness and this constituted the major hurdle for a small boy. That shining floor looked for all the world like the surface of an ice skating rink.

Lying there as I was in bed, swathed in blankets and covers, I would fancy that a trip to the bathroom was like a venture across snowy wastes to the North Pole. But the vital moment would come when I summoned all my strength, flung back the bedclothes, jumped out of bed and took off like a startled rabbit across the floor. That move, that action, launched me into a new day with all its possibilities and potentialities.

DECISIVE MOTIVATIONAL ACTION #2

Take your decisive action as a means toward a goal, being aware of the factors that can make you into a no-goer or a slow-goer; determine to be a go-goer. The mechanics of personality that make addiction possible offer you the potential of the considerable assistance of a positive addiction.

The action an individual takes in connection with the plan of this book is an adventure in faith that will lead into new experiences and pathways in life.

This action is never an end in itself; it leads on somewhere else. If it is to be effective this first step must be undertaken with the realization that *it is going to lead* elsewhere.

In their response to the action premise people can be divided into three groups.

The No-Goers

London is thought by many to be the most interesting city in the world. It has many attractions, but the most outstanding of these is certainly not automobile travel. Those ancient streets are a maze; one taxi driver told me it took three years to pass an examination on the shortest route from place to place within the city. The traffic congestion and parking problems are so monumental that knowledgeable people take to the superb underground railway as the best means of transportation around the city.

Trying to cope with the horrendous parking problems, the city struggled with the difficulty of parking violators. Tickets can be ignored, particularly in such a large city, and the practice of towing away is immeasurably complicated by the density of the traffic.

In 1983 the authorities came up with the "Denver Boot" as a solution to the problem of parking violations. It works this way. When a car is in violation of parking regulations a policeman arrives with the bright yellow-colored Denver Boot. He attaches this device to one wheel of the vehicle and locks it in place, and places on the window glass of the vehicle a notice announcing, "This vehicle has been immobilized." The special notice instructs the violator to report to the police station and adds a warning of the penalty for any attempt to move the vehicle.

The very word automobile means a "self-propelled, self-moving vehicle," and the Denver Boot is attached to deprive the car of its primary function as a means of locomotion. This is rather like human beings. As we will shortly notice, the very essence of life itself is movement, but some elements within our society do everything they can to deny the very movement that is so essential.

When I first became interested in physical fitness, I decided I would kill two birds with the one stone and save gasoline while getting fit. I would walk the three miles between my home and the office. My main problem was with well-intentioned motorists who constantly stopped to offer me a ride. They could not imagine why anyone would walk when he had the opportunity to ride.

This American society in which so much has been accomplished by action and hard work has lost its faith in muscle power and feels the mark of success is to be able to sit back and take it easy. The message is so frequently repeated that the general population absorbs the idea and the life of idleness and ease becomes the desirable goal. So we develop individuals who try to be like the lotus eaters of Grecian mythology, who lived on the flowers of the jujube tree and entered into a world of sweet indifference. This land of the lotus eaters is almost an experience of oblivion.

The NO-GOER is one of the living dead.

The Slow-Goers

There was no doubt in the mind of John Wesley, the founder of the Methodist Church, as to the importance of family religion. It was, he said, "The grand desideratum among Methodists." He tells in his journal of being delighted when many of those who heard him in London "... adopted Joshua's resolution, 'As for me and my house, we will serve the Lord.'"

Concerned about the future of the great revival of religion then taking place in England, he pondered the future. He noted that it might fulfill Martin Luther's "melancholy" premonition that "a revival of religion never lasts more than one generation."

As Wesley saw it, the answer to this problem was to give close attention to the rising generation and to focus on the family. In this family there were to be priorities. Wesley stated it very clearly to the males of his day, "The person in your house that claims your first and nearest attention is your wife."

All of these considerations would lead us to believe that Wesley, who had grown up in the midst of an unusual family, with a remarkable mother he obviously adored, and who was constantly telling parents how to raise their offspring, would have married and raised a family of unusual children.

But he did not and the reason was that in the arena of marriage he was a Slow-Goer.

What has been called Wesley's lost love involved a sea captain's widow named Grace Murray. Following her conversion, this gifted woman joined a Methodist society where she soon demonstrated unusual leadership ability in working with groups and relating to people. She became one of Wesley's assistants and was so valuable to him that he referred to her as "my right arm."

Following an illness in which Grace cared for him, Wesley raised the possibility of marriage. He later went as far as entering a betrothal agreement. But he could never get around to finalizing the formal marriage arrangements.

Almost incredibly the relationship dragged on for ten years. Busy with his work, Wesley constantly found reasons for delay—a necessity to consult with his preachers, the reduction of the antipathy of many of the women in the societies toward Grace, and the objections of his brother Charles to such a marriage.

Tired of all this waiting around (and who could really blame her after ten years of vacillation on Wesley's part),

Grace finally ran off with and married John Bennet, one of Wesley's preachers.

In the British Museum in London there is a little black book, the copy of a long account of Wesley's agony over the loss of Grace Murray.

If we have faith in the hereditary factors in families, what a tragedy it was that John Wesley had no children; and the main reason was that, as far as family life was concerned, he was a *Slow-Goer*.

Families are such dynamic developing units that action must be taken at the teachable moment or else the opportunity will be forever missed. There is no place in the vital family unit for the *Slow-Goer*.

The Go-Go Group

A strange new concern has come upon the American public in the discovery of the modern scourge of killer stress. This concern has led some to call our present era the Age of Stress. The one man most responsible for creating this perception is probably the late Dr. Hans Selye, sometimes referred to as "Dr. Stress."

Although the concept of stress has been widely discussed, few have taken the time to examine what Selye had to say about it. As he saw it, there are three types of stress—hypostress, stress, and eustress.

HYPOSTRESS   STRESS   EUSTRESS

Each of us probably has his or her own definition of stress, if we were to take the time to define it. Dr. Selye has been quoted as saying that stress is "the body's nonspecific response to any demand placed on it, whether that demand is pleasant or not." This primitive reaction to threat is sometimes called the "fight or flight" mechanism and leads the reactor into a variety of experiences.

Eustress is the enjoyable type of stress. Selye illustrated this by contrasting the stress which comes from sitting in a dentist's chair and that which one experiences when passionately kissing a pretty girl. The first is stress, the latter eustress.

Hypostress, said Selye, is the condition of too little stress. It is characterized by an absence of activity. Selye was skeptical about the value of many of the techniques for dealing with stress which call for idleness and meditation.

Psychiatrist Beach agrees with Selye and says, "There is no such thing as living totally free from stress. Just staying alive creates stress. Those under no stress are in the graveyard." Complete absence of stress is not the true objective of life.

Selye divided people into two categories: "racehorses," who thrive on a fast, vigorous life, and "turtles," who must have a tranquil environment. He readily admitted that he belonged to the "racehorse" category and said, "I could hardly imagine any worse torture than having to lie on a beach doing nothing day after day; yet, in my travels, I've noticed a great number of people whose chief aim in life is to be able to do precisely that."[4]

Many knowledgeable people would willingly back up Selye in his position. One of these is William Glasser who postulates what he calls Positive Addiction. The criteria he sets down for this experience of Positive Addiction are:

1. It is something noncompetitive that you choose to do and can devote an hour (approximately) a day to.

2. It is possible for you to do it easily and does not require a great deal of mental effort to do it well.

3. It does not depend upon others; you can do it alone or (rarely) with others.

4. You believe for you it has some value—physical, mental, or spiritual.

5. You believe that if you persist in it you will improve, but this is completely subjective—you need to be the only one who measures that improvement.

6. The activity must be of such a character that you can do it without criticizing yourself. If you can't accept yourself during this time, the activity will not be addicting.[5]

This last element may be the all-important consideration. I want you to feel good about your role as a "go-go" actionist. Don't worry about what other people think of your activity; it will pay dividends for you.

This happy group of actionists are up and ready to go. They have eager eyes and an enthusiastic spirit, and are the joy of a leader's heart. Their reward is twofold: They have the joyful subjective experience and their enthusiasm is so infectious that other people are influenced by them.

We will see later on that some very good evidence shows that the body itself, which is made for movement, functions at a higher level when kept in motion. The plus comes with some of the by-products of this movement such as the secretion of hormones which make the body more tolerant of pain and give the individual a natural high.

But preeminently Go-Goers do something to themselves and set in motion forces within their own personalities that have a cumulative effect on them. Their acting in a situation not only influences their circumstances but affects the doer. He is changed into a different individual.

A Positively-Addicted Mother

One of the not so obvious areas for positive addiction is the family. But an excellent example of a family "addict" would be Susanna Wesley, the mother of John and Charles Wesley.

Susanna had a wide experience of family life, being one of twenty-five children herself. She bore nineteen children. Wife of a Church of England minister, she managed on an inadequate salary, looked after the glebe lands belonging to the parish, took part in church activities, and for twenty years ran what must have been a full-time school.

She taught her children, using what she described as "my method." With the household ordered so no one would interrupt the process she and the children settled down to work. She taught each child the alphabet in one day and then set an open Bible on the table and, beginning at the book of Genesis, taught a word at a time until the child could read a whole verse. From that she worked with each one until he or she could read a whole chapter.

A strict disciplinarian, she laid down specific rules for her children which she spelled out in a later letter to her most famous son:

1. Even as babies they were taught to cry softly.
2. The children had to eat whatever was put before them.
3. They were not allowed to eat or drink between meals.
4. All children were to be in bed by 8 P.M.
5. Each child had to be obedient because self-will was the root of all sin and misery.
6. Once a child had been punished the event was forgotten and never held against the child.

Susanna's positive addiction to family can be seen in her willingness to go to great lengths in her teaching method. On one occasion her husband, watching her working with the children, marveled and said, "I wonder at your patience; you have told that child the same thing twenty times."

She calmly replied, "If I had satisfied myself by mentioning it only nineteen I should have lost all my labor. It was the twentieth time that crowned it." This skillful teacher demonstrated that repetition breeds retention.

And through it all she demonstrated her concern for the individual. She said, "I observe the following method. I take such a proportion of time I can spare every night to discourse with each child. On Monday I talk with Molly, Tuesday with Hetty, Wednesday with Nancy, Thursday with Jacky, Friday with Patty, Saturday with Charles, and with Emily and Sukey together on Sunday."

Small wonder she produced a John and a Charles Wesley. These are the rewards of those positively addicted to family life.

One of the most widely used measures of stress is the Social Adjustment Rating Scale which came as a result of the work of Holmes and Rahe. The top three events on this scale which indicated the probability of stress all have to do with family life. For Susanna the events of family life were *eustress* and gave zest and flavor to the whole of living.

Try a Little Self-examination

Do you fit into one of these three categories? If you do, what action should you take?

1. Are you a no-goer?
Face your peril. If movement is the sign of life, then you

are in mortal danger. Think of aircraft. Lighter-than-air craft still occasionally float lazily across the sky, but they are expensive, slow, bulky, and above all, vulnerable and dangerous. Heavier-than-air craft operate on the principle that movement gives lift, enabling them to soar into the upper atmosphere. Float if you will. Live your sluggish existence. You will be vulnerable physically and emotionally.

2. Are you a slow-goer?

Nothing is ever accomplished without enthusiasm. Comedian Red Skelton, who has made so many of us laugh for so many years, has given us a tongue-in-cheek version of action (and unwittingly encouraged the slow-goers and given comfort to the indolent) by saying that the main exercise he gets these days is serving as a pallbearer at the funerals of his exercising friends.

It is easy to develop such rationalizations for lack of action, but you are going to pay the ultimate penalty. *You need the message of this book.* Let the reading of this volume be the first action that you take. Keep an open mind as you read and you will make some interesting discoveries as you go.

3. Are you a go-goer?

Congratulations. Keep on with your good work. This volume will be an affirmation of your commitment to the joy of living as an actionist. You will find that the actionist discovers ever widening opportunities for utilizing the action premise and in this volume you will be introduced to a number of new areas where you can apply the action principle.

The Animal Within Us All

One of the hobbies I enjoy is brass rubbings. While making copies from grave markers of English nobility of the fourteenth to the eighteenth centuries, I was surprised at how many men were depicted in the company of their dogs. Sometimes the animal was portrayed at his owner's feet; in other instances, in a ridiculous draping posture around the master's shoulders.

This penchant of human beings toward a relationship with animals has carried over to the practice of likening people to various members of the animal kingdom. Dr. Johnson, for example, referred to John Wesley as "that dog Wesley." Some women have been unkindly referred to as "catty"; an indecent man might be called "horsey"; a sharp-witted person, "foxy"; or a pugnacious individual, a "bull-dog."

When it comes to action two animals represent the extremes of approaches to movement. One is the sloth. This South American native is an ugly creature with no tail or ears, coarse hair, and peg-like teeth. It lives its life in the treetops, generally upside down, seeming to lack the energy to get right side up. It spends its day in sleep and inches about in the darkness.

The sloth's movement is slow, slow, slow. When it infrequently decides to move, its top "speed" is about a third of a mile an hour. The sloth is easy prey for many predators; its slowness of movement has given the English language the word slothful.

The major enemy of the sloth is the jungle cat, which serves to remind us of the other extreme in movement, the cheetah, the most effective hunter in the cat family. The cheetah is a beautiful animal with a small head. Its compressed body reduces wind resistance. Its feet have hard pads, and claws with no sheaths, thus facilitating its great speed. A long tail apparently is a factor in its capacity for turning very quickly. Known for its hunting prowess, in hot pursuit of prey the cheetah can move at speeds up to seventy miles per hour.

Called "the fastest land animal in the world," the cheetah is playful, friendly, and relatively easily trained, and has never been known to attack a human being. When contented the cheetah will purr like a house cat. It is a useful predator that plays an important role in the life cycle of the animal world.

To call a man an "animal" is usually seen as a rebuke, but a more appropriate response might be, "Which animal?"

If our action premise be correct, and it surely is, the most insulting response will be, a sloth, the most complimentary, a cheetah. Decide which you want to be: the sloth hiding in the treetops, avoiding the light of day, waiting for the cover of night to make a slow, tentative move—the person the Bible refers to as the sluggard—or the cheetah, the actionist, purposeful, attractive, moving, adventurous, achieving.

THE CHOICE IS YOURS!

Why Not Become Positively Addicted?

Recall the criteria of positive addiction:

1. Something noncompetitive to which you can devote an hour a day.
2. It doesn't require a great deal of mental effort.
3. You can do it on your own.
4. It yields some physical, mental, or spiritual value for you.
5. If you persist in it, you will improve.
6. You do not have to be self-critical.

It's Your Move

Think carefully about this. Remember, you have the forces of your own body working for you. What certain something is there that you would really like to concentrate on? Make your decision. Go to it.

Think carefully about this. Remember, you have the forces of your own body working for you. What certain something is there that you would really like to concentrate on? Make your decision. Go to it.

3
How to Escape
From the "I Can't" Trap

The type of action advocated here is initiated by the actionist. He does not just drift into it. He makes a deliberate choice. When a certain point is reached the actionist makes a definite commitment and becomes involved by taking a DECISIVE MOTIVATIONAL ACTION.

Methods of entering the swimming pool provide an example. One way of undertaking this task is to gingerly approach the pool and slowly unwrap. Then move to the edge and dip in one toe. The next move is to slowly walk toward the steps and to enter the water step by step, pausing at each level. The water level creeps up—ankles, shins, knees, buttocks, chest, and at long last, the neck—until the head is still held bravely above the water. Such an agonizing entry transforms what should have been an exhilarating experience into what could be more appropriately called water torture.

The other method is to walk briskly to the edge of the pool and dive in, coming up tingling with a sensation of being alive, flooded with the joy and exhilaration of living.

This is the way of the Decisive Motivational Action. You can't do it by inches.

Miss Marsh, the head nurse of a ward in a hospital in Australia, demonstrated this for me. This lady, though un-married, certainly knew how to handle men, as I found to my dismay.

DECISIVE MOTIVATIONAL ACTION #3

Face the fact that the attitude of "I can't" must be changed to "I won't" to realize the potentialities of the life of an actionist. Tak-ing one single decisive action may lead you into a whole new era of experience.

I had the misfortune of fracturing my femur and the fur-ther misfortune of being subjected to an enthusiastic but in-experienced young intern in the hospital. He decided to cover my injured leg from thigh to the sole of my foot with adhesive tape. The task completed, my leg looked as if it had been borrowed from an Egyptian mummy.

The Tape-Rip Principle

Then came the orthopedic surgeon whose verdict was that the situation called for surgery. The tape had to be removed and an aide apologetically started on the job. I writhed in agony and protested every inch of tape as she tried to remove it ever so gingerly. Then head nurse Marsh happened by. She made a quick decision. "Turn your face to the wall," she ordered. That done, she took the loosened end of one piece of tape and suddenly gave it a mighty yank. I felt as if it were the end of the world.

So it proceeded—her yanking punctuated with my fierce impassioned protests and her heartless commands, "Turn to the wall." The job finally completed, I lay there contemplating my hairless, reddened, tenderized leg. My only consolation came in realizing that what might have required a half hour of protracted misery was over and done with in a mere five minutes.

Miss Marsh had taught me the valuable lesson of the decisive action. But it was *her* action. I later learned the lesson of the decisive action which I personally need to take.

Write It in Blood

I am thinking of Brother Hammel, a wonderful elderly Scotsman and faithful deacon in his church who never missed an opportunity to give a testimony of his Christian experience. He would recount the time when as a boy in Scotland he made the most important commitment of his life, accepting Christ as his own personal Savior. The occasion was so significant for him that he opened a vein in his arm, dipped the point of a pen in his blood and recorded his decision on the front page of the Bible he so proudly carried under his arm to church. Whenever I hear the expression "written in blood" I think of Brother Hammel.

This is the type of commitment I am calling for. It begins

with a commitment of faith in Christ which in turn demands a life of action.

Don't Say You *Can't* When You Mean *Won't*

Of course there are always those who put a pathetic look on their face and say, "I think that is wonderful, and in many ways I would like to commit myself to some line of action, but I can't." They make this statement with a look on their face which seems to indicate that they are suffering with some horrible disease which has completely immobilized them and makes it impossible for them to do what they would so much like to.

This situation seems to disarm the would-be motivator until he makes contact with some of the students of the human psyche. The followers of Fritz Perls who call their theory Gestalt Therapy are used to situations like this. Some people are in deep trouble because they are mired down and wallowing in their misery. The Perls technique is confrontive and often involves focusing attention on one person who is on the "hot seat." As he is urged to try some line of behavior, the subject frequently says, "I can't do that."

The response is, "Please say that again, only change the wording a little; say, 'I *won't* do that.' "

In a moment the defense has been attacked and the client compelled to face his unwillingness to act.

In this book you are going to be confronted with a series of situations in which you need to undertake some actions. One of your immediate reactions is going to be, "I can't do that."

Change your statement and say, "I WON'T DO THAT." Let it be a *decisive* motivational action.

Grace Murray Hopper is one of the outstanding women in

America today. But when she is presiding over a conference she refuses to be referred to by the non-sexist term of "the chair." She prefers the traditional term of chairman despite its alleged sexist connotation.

Why? She replies, "I won't be an 'inanimate object'! That stuff's all nonsense. It gets us nowhere."[6]

She is certainly no "inanimate object." At seventy-eight years of age she is the oldest officer in the U.S. Navy and was recently promoted to the rank of commodore. Her list of achievements is staggering. Retired from the navy at sixty years of age—"The saddest day of my life"—she was called back into service to help in her specialized field of computers. She wrote COBOL, a widely-used computer language.

Commodore Hopper was the first person to use a now universal word to describe a glitch that interferes with the computer's functioning. While working on a malfunction in a computer she discovered an errant moth had become entangled in the circuitry and described the problem as a "bug."

This remarkable woman, affectionately known as "the grand old lady of software," is an actionist. She maintains that some actions must be taken no matter what the cost.

"It's easier to apologize than it is to get permission," she says. One of her favorite sayings is, "A ship in port is safe, but that is not what ships are built for." Preeminent to her are human decisions. She has unbounded confidence in computers second only to the people who run them and take the Decisive Motivational Action. Her judgment is that "Apollo would never have come back to earth, despite the computers on board, if men had not been there to make the decisions."

When five hundred specialists in the field of family life

were queried as to what they considered to be the fifteen traits characteristic of good wholesome family life, one of their responses was: a good family exhibits a sense of shared responsibility.

A mother told of the time when one of her children wrote "dust me" on the top of the television set and she took that as a signal that the child was old enough to accept responsibility. She gave him the job of dusting the living room. Congratulations, mother!

A successful modern family demands flexibility and responsibility—a *shared* responsibility which must be accepted by all the members of the family.

The Single Action That Saved a Family

A Tale of Two Men might have been an appropriate title for the book, *A Tale of Two Cities,* for it tells the age-old story of two men who love the same Lucie Manette. Sydney Carton was a failed man who had not used his brilliant legal mind purposefully. Rather, he lived his life in a backwater, wasting his talents.

Of Carton the author said there was no sadder sight. This man of good abilities, incapable of using them, resigned himself to letting his blight destroy his magnificent gifts.

But his love of Lucie Manette was ever before Sydney Carton. He watched his rival for her affections, Charles Darnay, woo and win Lucie, and become the father of her two children. Then came his opportunity as Darnay returned to France at the height of the revolution. There he was captured and sentenced to death at the guillotine.

All Carton had to do was to let events take their course and his rival would be removed. Then, in time, he could achieve all that he longed for. But the image of that family was before Carton and he concluded that he must take action. Because of his uncanny resemblance to Lucie's husband Charles Darnay, Carton was able to take Darnay's place and be guillotined in his stead.

Carton had a vision before his eyes of seeing the little family living out their lives as a happy unit. His last words summarized the attitude of a man who realized that the preservation of a family was more important than his gaining his own personal satisfaction: "It is a far, far better thing that I do, than I have ever done."

The indolent Carton had made his great resolution which launched him into an action that saved a family and transformed him from a failure to a hero without parallel in literature. All because of a Decisive Motivational Action.

IT IS A FAR, FAR BETTER THING THAT I DO
THAN I HAVE EVER DONE

4
Move Your Body

Absolute inactivity is death.
Daniel J. Leithauser

The more medically-minded refer to a dead human as a "cadaver." To me this sounds rather like a reference to some nonhuman species. An undertaker I once knew would sometimes startle loved ones by asking what they wanted to do with "the remains." This isn't any better than cadaver, suggesting as it does the leftovers from a meal which might be kept in the refrigerator.

The vague reference to "the departed" contains at least an inference that he might just be "out for lunch." "Corpse" has a certain ominous note to it. All things being considered, for me, the most accurate, graphic and descriptive word is the colloquialism, "stiff." This word sums up the essential difference between life and death.

Movement Versus Rest As Healer

As a youth I spent some months in a hospital. I had fractured my thigh and, following a period with my leg in a special splint suspended from a frame over the bed, there came
a long spell of recuperation. I was still confined to bed, with
my limb encased in a plaster cast.

A ten-year-old boy in the bed next to me had a similar in-
jury to mine, but he refused to obey the doctor's edict to remain still. The day his leg was put in plaster he inveigled an
orderly into getting him a pair of crutches and sneaked outside.

DECISIVE MOTIVATIONAL ACTION #4

Because movement is the sign and indicator
of life, the human body needs motion. To
function at its best, it should be moved rather
than rested. Absolute inactivity is death and
to ward off the Grim Reaper we must involve
ourselves in a program of physical activity.

A week or so later the ten-year-old electrified the whole
hospital community when a nurse espied him, plaster cast
and all, at the top of a thirty-foot tree. I speculated that the
kid would come to a sticky end and finish up with a pretzel-
shaped limb. But within a few months the boy was playing
soccer, while I limped to the outpatient department to have
my stiffened knee manipulated. I finally finished up with an
arthritic condition which bothered me for many years.

The Way Kids and Animals Do It

The boy with the broken leg is typical of so many children who refuse to stay still like "good children." Reports come of nurses driven to distraction by small fry, recently having undergone surgery, crawling around, standing, playing games, climbing over the end of the bed and making re-markable recoveries.

Experimenters have noted the same phenomenon with animals. After some types of surgery, the animal refuses to re-main still, gets up, wanders around, takes a few periods of rest, and eats and drinks in a normal manner. Strange as it may seem to the followers of the rest-and-recover regimen, their wounds from the surgery heal remarkably well.

The Patient Who Refused to Obey Doctor's Orders

Dr. Daniel J. Leithauser's thirty-eight-year-old patient, with scant respect for medical authority, insisted on fre-quently leaving his bed just a few hours after the removal of his appendix. Despite warnings about possible dire results, he departed from the hospital on the following day.

The next day the patient took a thirty-mile drive into the downtown area of the city. On the third and fourth days fol-lowing surgery he went to work in his garden. Then he fol-lowed that by taking a journey of forty miles to the doctor's office for an examination which showed him to be in excel-lent condition.

Considering this patient, the thoughtful doctor launched himself on a quest to discover the relationship between early ambulation and healing. Starting from the conviction that nature is the real healer, he postulated that the surgeon's task is to provide the conditions under which nature can work. He concluded that the best way to cooperate with nature is to involve the patient in activity and have him rise from bed as soon as possible after surgery.

The surgeon later discovered that a certain Emil Rise of Chicago, nearly fifty years before, had undertaken a similar investigation and had concluded that the patient should not remain in bed, but rise and become active. Unfortunately, the insights of this pioneer researcher had been largely ignored.

Dr. Leithauser not only practiced the action principle which he called "early ambulation," but continued to gather evidence of the validity of his thesis. He gave a questionnaire to 667 former patients and out of these, 651 said that if they had another operation they would prefer to get out of bed early again.

Patients Should Have No Choice but Early Ambulation

From his research Dr. Leithauser became so convinced of the merits of patients rising from bed on the day after surgery that he declared, "It is important not because it *can* be done, but because it *must* be done." This led to his classical formulation, "The patient should have no choice as to early ambulation."[7]

Studies of animals produced significant confirming results. Researchers took 120 adult white rats, made identical incisions on them and uniformly stitched up their wounds. Sixty of the rats were confined to stationary cages with only limited possibilities for movement. The second group of sixty were placed in rotatable cages where they could engage in unrestricted activity.

Movement Is the Sign and Indicator of Life

The experiment proved that the wounds of the active animals had superior tensile strength, giving evidence that activity not only did not hurt but actually facilitated the healing process.

At a time when hospital costs are soaring, the concept of early ambulation has some intriguing possibilities. In an issue of *International Surgery,* Dr. Carol J. Bellis reported his commitment to the action premise.[8] He reported 11,272 inguinal hernia repairs performed over a period of twenty-nine years. His technique involved using a local anaesthetic, shaving a small area, and making a small incision. The patient ate breakfast before surgery, sat up for lunch, and walked out of the hospital fully clothed in the afternoon.

In marked contrast to the careful regimen of hernia patients who are not even permitted to drive a car for weeks after surgery, Dr. Bellis's patients were permitted unrestricted swimming, tennis, golf or work. From his observation of all these cases, Bellis concluded, "There is virtually no prospect of infection or wound separation."

Although proclaimed by many as a pioneer, Bellis liked to recall that Ephraim McDowell, a frontier surgeon of Kentucky, operated on Jane Todd Crawford in 1809 to remove a 22-pound ovarian tumor. Five days after surgery, Jane Todd made up her bed, and three weeks later mounted her horse to ride sixty miles home!

Move It or Lose It

Despite all the evidence of the past, circumstance and not theory pushed the practice of early ambulation to the fore.

During the German aerial attacks on England in World War II, patients could not be hospitalized for long periods of time. The hospital staff got patients out of bed and on their feet immediately following surgery and discharged them to their homes. The results were so good that these experiences of necessity gave fresh emphasis to the idea of "early ambulation."

With so many advantages coming from early ambulation after surgery one might imagine that the whole medical fraternity would have rushed to embrace the idea. But you have only to read a book like Leithauser's *Early Ambulation* to sense the resistance to the idea within the medical profession.

Commenting on the habit of prescribing bed rest, the perceptive doctor took on an ironic attitude and remarked, "The regenerative and healing forces of nature are so great, however, despite all the interferences to recovery that surgeons and physicians can devise."

Miseducation and Education

One of the main hindrances to the wide acceptance of early ambulation has been the fears of patients who frequently resist the idea. Leithauser claims this is a consequence of education by the medical profession. Education has been too good at promoting the idea of the importance of bed rest. This surgeon proposed a Decisive Motivation Action:

- The surgeon and staff should undertake an educational program with the patients.
- During their discussion of the subject with patients, the surgeon and staff should use expressions that emphasize benefits of early rising after surgery, such as:

"Helps you avoid blood clots."

"Keep your muscles in good shape."

"Enables you to cough up the secretions in your lungs to prevent the possibility of pneumonia."

- The title of Dr. Bellis's paper shows his commitment: "Immediate Unrestricted Activity after Operation."

At the level of the body, the action principle is of fundamental importance. Activity is the sign and indicator of life. Conversely, in Leithauser's words, "Absolute inactivity is death."

Begin with the Body

The action principle, of necessity, begins with the body. Humans are not disembodied spirits. They have bodies which are the vehicles through which they express themselves and interact with the surrounding world. Our bodies are such an important part of our human existence that the way in which this intricate mechanism functions will, to a large measure, determine our effectiveness in all our relationships.

When the body encounters difficulties it has an unusual capacity to repair itself. It has been the practice in the past to imagine that the therapeutic potentialities might be enhanced by rest, but now we know that this is not necessarily so.

At the center of the body is the remarkable little pump we call the heart. Keeping this heart in good condition turns out to be far simpler than we might have imagined and involves the debunking of a lot of widely-held ideas. These concepts will be considered in our next chapter.

All the evidence indicates that the body is made to move and is kept at the peak of its functioning by action. But not just any action. A planned program.

How to Make Your Heart Love You

If you haven't done anything for your heart lately, start now. Exercise it. It'll love you for it.

Kenneth H. Cooper

Watch out Pheidippides! Cooper is coming!

As every schoolboy used to know, Pheidippides was the young Greek who ran from Marathon to Athens, a distance of twenty-two miles, 1,470 yards, to carry the news of the Athenian victory. He stumbled into the city of Athens and declared, "Rejoice, we conquer!" Then he fell and died.

Inspired by this feat, the marathon—the most prestigious of all foot races, now standardized at 26 miles, 385 yards—was made a part of the Olympic Games. With the immense popularity of the marathon today, it could fairly be said that Pheidippides inspired more people to go racing against each other than did any other mortal.

That is, until Cooper came.

Dr. Kenneth Cooper's performance in motivating people to run is enough to cause Pheidippides to halt in his tracks and pull his chaplet down over his eyes in dismay. Cooper has been responsible for motivating more people (some claim as many as eight million Americans in addition to great numbers in other countries, of all ages) to embark on a running program than has any other human.

As for the possibility that what happened to Pheidippides might befall his modern-day counterpart, Cooper thumbs his nose at that. He has assembled an amazing array of technological devices—treadmills, electrocardiograms, water tanks—all of which are overseen by physicians who can call a halt at any moment when an exerciser gets into a danger zone.

Easy Does It

But before you go jogging down the street, mount your stationary cycle intent on pushing it to the limit, or take the plunge on your 700-yard swim, take note that Dr. Cooper insists you do it gradually. A 50-year-old man who wants to undertake a swimming program starts by swimming 100 yards in 2 minutes and 30 seconds, 5 times a week, to accumulate 4 points for his effort. It will take him 15 weeks to move gradually up to swimming 700 yards in 16 minutes and 30 seconds to reach the desirable level of 30 of Cooper's aerobic points.

Cooper's aerobic exercise program calls for action—strenuous exercise. He pours out his scorn on the programs that suggest that thirty minutes a week will do it. "It's an impossibility to develop total cardiovascular and pulmonary fitness in thirty minutes a week," he declares. Propagators of such programs, he says, are doing a disservice to a person who wants to use exercise as preventive medicine.

The Big Five

Though he is completely sold on the value of exercise, he does not esteem all forms of exercise as equal. To be effective an exercise must develop the exerciser's aerobic capacity, that is, increase the amount of oxygen his body can process in a given time. While he does calisthenics himself, he sees them as part of a total exercise program. Cooper has developed a hierarchy of exercises which have the best aerobic conditioning potential. They are, in descending order:

Cross-country skiing
Swimming
Jogging or running

Outdoor cycling

Walking

Probably Cooper's greatest contribution to the world of physical exercise is the technique he has developed for quantifying the amount of exercise an individual needs. He does this with a points system. In this system, a "conditioned person" does enough exercise to earn him thirty points a week. To do this, an individual may walk 3 miles in 45 minutes 4 times a week, swim 800 yards in 20 minutes 4 times a week, or run 2 miles in 22 minutes 4 times a week. He has extended the idea to a number of different exercises and provided guides for people at different age levels.

How Does It Work?

From all that Cooper is saying, it turns out that the secret to all this is a gas, a gas as free as the air we breathe. Air is comprised approximately of 21 percent oxygen and 79 percent nitrogen. The big problem is for the body to extract the oxygen from the air.

The beginning point is the lungs. They must draw in large quantities of air for processing. Cooper likens the lungs to a milk processing plant where the raw milk is delivered and cream is separated from it, bottled and prepared for delivery. Oxygen, the "cream" of the air we breathe, is bottled in red blood cells and sent off for delivery by the blood stream.

Having deposited the oxygen, the red blood cells pick up the carbon dioxide and other wastes from the tissue cells, proceed through the veins and back to the lungs where the carbon dioxide is exhaled with the expired air.

The All-Important "Training Effect"

Cooper's point in all this is to show the role of action in the functioning of the system. The "training effect," as he calls the results of an exercise program, produces more blood, more red blood cells, more hemoglobin, and more blood plasma. This results in a greater capacity for delivering oxygen and a more rapid return and expulsion of wastes. Cooper concludes concerning the circulatory system: "Increase its work load and it increases its efficiency. Sit around and do nothing, and it deteriorates. It's as simple as that."

THE MORE WORK YOU GIVE YOUR HEART
THE BETTER IT FUNCTIONS

At the center of all this intricate operation is a magnificent pump that sends the oxygen-filled blood from the lungs and forces it through the body. The condition of this remarkable instrument, which we call the heart, is all important. Dr. Cooper points out one of the strange anomalies. "Ironically, the heart works faster and less efficiently when you give it little to do than it does when you make more demands upon it. It is a remarkable engine."

Cooper suggests some conditions which most people would find highly desirable. They include:

- Higher levels of energy for longer periods during the day.
- Improved digestion and control of constipation.
- A realistic way to lose and control weight.
- Bones that will continue to be strong and healthy as age increases.

- Improved intellectual capacity and increased productivity.
- Better and more effective sleep.
- A very effective way to control depression and other emotional disturbances.
- Relief from stress at the end of a pressure-packed day without resorting to alcohol or drugs.
- Significant added protection from heart disease.[9]

All of these benefits can be had by anyone who is willing to spend as little as one hour and twenty minutes a week on a simple exercise program. But it must be done regularly and consistently.

I am writing this book on a computer and as I type on the keyboard the text appears on the screen. While my computer is turned on, this material will remain available as it is in the RAM—Random Access Memory—but if I do not go through the procedure known as "saving" this material onto a disk, it will disappear the moment I turn off the machine. I will have lost it. Physical fitness is something like that. It cannot be stored. Within just a few days after quitting exercise we begin to lose the benefits. We must keep on with our program.

The Benefits of a Physical Action Program

Exercise may be the closest thing we have to a panacea for the ills that beset the human frame. It is the prescription without the medicine, the mood elevator without the drugs, the pickup without the hangover, the weight control without the diet, the cosmetic found in no drugstore, the sedative without a chemical, the tranquilizer without a pill, the indicator of life without a cardiogram, the therapy more effective than any psychiatrist's couch, the cure for depression without a fee, the fountain of life without a legend.

The actionist discovers that at what might be considered the lowest level of functioning, the physical, the action principle opens up possibilities of joyous and meaningful living.

Six Decisive Motivational Actions

1. Don't overlook the possibilities for exercise in ordinary, everyday activities—walking to work, using the stairs instead of the elevator. When you go shopping, try reaching down to the lower shelves, twisting, carrying the sack of groceries.

2. A good program of exercise requires a decisive motivational effort of at least twenty minutes a day. Four or five minutes a day will not do it.

3. Develop your program gradually.

4. Exercise regularly. One study showed that daily exercise is best, with one day a week for rest. Even as little as three nonconsecutive days of exercise a week will maintain an adequate level of fitness.

5. Exercise sensibly. If your breathing has not returned to normal within five to ten minutes after exercising you may be overdoing it.

6. Buy the book, *The Aerobics Program for Total Well-Being* by Dr. Kenneth H. Cooper. It is superb.

The Aerobic Family

Cooper suggests that to all the terms that we use about the family—the traditional family, the extended family, the nuclear family—add another, the aerobic family. He adds that the family that exercises together "frequently possesses a much greater level of well-being and unity."

It all needs to begin with the parents who become the

model for their children. Exercise may be an important factor in the relationship of husband and wife. Some exercises lend themselves to a combined effort. My wife and I went through a period when we enjoyed cycling. After a while on individual bicycles we invested in a tandem and discovered some side benefits, such as learning to cooperate and communicate in handling the tandem bike. We had already come to appreciate the benefits of getting up earlier and of the warm glow of exercise.

Then there is the joy of walking, an exercise that one can engage in anywhere. On a recent trip to Europe we walked around the airport, climbed a mountain, traversed through the parks. In Germany we joined in several *volksmarches*, wonderful events drawing dozens of people, including families. They walk about six miles and receive a medal or some other form of recognition. On our return flight we discovered a way to walk a mile around the gigantic 747 airliner as we flew across the Atlantic. Walking really gives a family a sense of togetherness.

Many benefits come to a family that attempts a good exercise program:

- Family togetherness.
- Happier homes, by providing a way for members to deal with the stress that threatens to disrupt the family.
- Longer life. As Dr. Leaf said, "Exercise is the closest thing we have to an antiaging pill."
- Lower medical expenses as the family practices one of the best forms of preventive medicine.
- Enhanced communication between parents and children, especially with teenagers.

MOVEMENT IS THE SIGN AND INDICATOR OF LIFE

5
Handcuff the Thief

On that hot day I stood, feeling rather like a sardine in a can, in the crowded standing space of the bus pressed against the bodies squeezed around me. The only movement came with the lurching of the vehicle, causing the human sardines to sway in unison.

There were two reasons for the excitement I was experiencing at that moment. I was in a bus identical to the ones I traveled in my native Australia, even to its double-decked configuration and red color, and we were progressing down a street in Hong Kong, one of the most colorful cities in the world.

In my euphoric moment I was blissfully unaware that I was on the verge of an experience which I would recall for many years to come.

The bus ground to a halt and began to disgorge passengers striving to disentangle themselves from the mass of bodies and struggle out onto the sidewalk. Suddenly a gentleman who had been patiently standing near me was galvanized into activity and shouted at the top of his voice, "That man has stolen my wallet. Grab him. Don't let him get away!"

Pandemonium broke loose as people called out, and struggled to grasp the offender who managed to break loose, fleeing down the street but dropping his booty as he ran. The man who had come close to losing his wallet turned out to be a missionary who had seen many years of service in the Orient. He explained, "I've learned that the moment you sense you've been fingered, it's best to do something, preferably raise a commotion."

As you read this, a thief is hard at work stealing our good name, our money, our internal peace of mind, our opportunities, and our time. His name—PROCRASTINATION. Worst of all, like many pickpocket victims, we don't know we've been robbed.

During my work as a professor in a graduate school it was necessary for me to interview students planning to do work at our highest level. Having reviewed their academic achievements, I would move into some of their more personal difficulties. I would note with pleasure their achievements, but I would ask each one what was his or her biggest area of failure.

To my great surprise I discovered their failures were not what I expected. These students whose work required them to meet many deadlines repeatedly told me that the problem that gave them their most difficulty was procrastination.

Apparently this process begins early in an individual's academic career. Reports from the schoolroom tell us that a new generation of students not only is learning the art of procrastinating to avoid their responsibilities, but has enlisted the aid of that box of electronic wizardry we call the computer. This remarkable machine has not only become an aid to learning, but has enhanced the craft of procrastinating by providing a whole raft of excuses for evading responsibility.

"My father was using the typewriter," has become, "My mother was using the peripherals." Instead of, "My brother scribbled on my work," it is, "My chiphead sister was playing squish and zonked my file." "I left my work on the kitchen table," has become, "I left my disk in the computer." And that almost universal rationalization from the business world has moved into the schoolroom—"The computer was down."

Whatever the terminology, it is still the language of procrastination, which indicates that for some procrastinators the main benefit of the computer revolution may be a whole group of new rationalizations with which to justify their tardiness.

The Mañana Test

Take this simple test and see if the thief, procrastination, is robbing you too. Check #1 if the statement is true of you *frequently*, #2 if the statement is true of you *sometimes*, #3 if *occasionally*, or #4 if *never*.

Do you say, "I've got my own priorities" and react defensively if it is suggested you're not good on deadlines?

1. _____ 2. _____ 3. _____ 4. _____

Do you adopt the attitude, "The South Americans have the right idea—*mañana*—tomorrow"?

1. _____ 2. _____ 3. _____ 4. _____

Do you enjoy spending a lot of time in trifling, insignificant matters and leave the big things unattended?

1. _____ 2. _____ 3. _____ 4. _____

As you approach a deadline do you say, "Everyone else will be late; why should I kill myself?"

1. _____   2. _____   3. _____   4. _____

Do you make a joke about it and say, "It's better late than never," when you have failed to meet a deadline?

1. _____   2. _____   3. _____   4. _____

Is it a practice of yours to say, "What's not done today can be done tomorrow"?

1. _____   2. _____   3. _____   4. _____

Do you see all the difficult aspects of a task and think of the bad ways it can turn out?

1. _____   2. _____   3. _____   4. _____

Do you congratulate yourself by saying, "I'm not going to get caught up in the rat race"?

1. _____   2. _____   3. _____   4. _____

PROCRASTINATION IS THE MAJOR FOE OF THE ACTION PRINCIPLE

How did you come out? Add the numbers to the right of your check marks and discover your procrastination ratio from the scale below.

Rating Your Procrastination Quotient

10–15 Serious procrastinator. You need to take urgent action.

16–20 Problem procrastinator. Consider your situation. Drop your excuses and rationalizations.

21–29 Periodic procrastinator. Beware of the down cycles. Aim at developing consistency.

30–40 You are doing well. Keep on.

Consider your Procrastination Ratio very carefully. There's a good chance you may have been surprised by the way in which you use this unprofitable technique for handling the situations of your life. Many people's lives have gotten out of control because of their procrastinating ways which lead them to postpone the action which could have made all the difference. Can you feel the stirrings within you that indicate you should do something about the situation? Procrastinate no longer.

Trick a Trickster

Let's face it—procrastination is a habit and it may be the very worst of all habits because it steals your most precious possession—time.

There's bad news and good news. The bad news is that procrastination can immobilize you and leave you like a spineless jellyfish. The good news is that there is a way out. We will consider a plan to break the habit of procrastination.

DECISIVE MOTIVATIONAL ACTION #5

Having discovered some of your losses, develop a plan of action for recovering your most valuable asset from the thief procrastination. Use a ten-step effort that will help you trick the trickster.

1. Remember the way to eat an elephant.

Cedrick Harrison has always loved the English language, playing word games and writing witty notes to his friends. After a trip abroad he wrote a letter to a friend who showed it to the editor of the local paper. The editor called Cedrick and received permission to publish the witty epistle.

Then came the offer of a weekly column. Cedrick commenced writing the column with great enthusiasm and his friends began to call him Hillsborough's Art Buchwald. After a month, during which he had increasing difficulty in getting around to writing, and kept the editor waiting, he said he was tired of the "rat race" and quit.

The editor took Cedrick out to lunch and had a serious talk with him about his writing, telling him that he was particularly good but apparently undisciplined. Pointing out how they had fallen over backwards to keep him writing, the editor concluded, "If you were to discipline yourself and keep on with the column, within a couple of years you could have a very fine book."

Cedrick thanked the editor, then explained: "Of course, I want to write, but I want to do it well. I need time to think, to play with ideas. When I make enough money to take a year off from my business I'll write a book that will set the literary world on its ears. I need time, time to do a good job, time to reflect."

Poor Cedrick. He will never write. The creative juices will never flow quite the way they do in the midst of much activity.

Thomas Gray sat in the graveyard of the Stoke Poges Anglican Church in England, and, looking over the graves, wrote: "Some mute inglorious Milton here may rest."

There's a good chance the man who had literary gifts but never used them was a procrastinator.

An author's secretary was once asked the secret of her busy boss's creativity. She responded, "He uses little pieces of time, fifteen minutes, sometimes five minutes, leaves it, then returns."

How do you eat an elephant?

One bite at a time.

Don't be overawed by the time the total job will take. Begin with the small segments. You'll be amazed at the way they will mount up. By doing the little tasks you will find your inertia will dissipate. You will suddenly discover you are spending increasingly longer periods of time at your task. Hear the word of one of the greatest authors of all time:

My advice is, never do tomorrow what you can do today. Procrastination is the thief of time. Collar him.

Charles Dickens

2. Try the "what if" method.

Joan Thompson has signed up for a college course on human relations and has been working hard on her assignments. Her paper on assertiveness training was the result of long hours of work, so she was disappointed to receive a B grade.

Her problem was that the professor had made a strong point about the difference between aggressiveness and assertiveness, and he had poured out his scorn on the "women's libbers" who, he said, were a denial of the beauty of femininity. If she approached him with a question about her grade, she feared he might think she was one of those "aggressive" females.

Joan showed her paper to several of her friends and they all agreed she should ask the professor to review the grade. But Joan vacillated; she began to get the feeling of being a martyr and found some consolation in her sufferings.

Jim, who worked with her, challenged her to do something. "Why not use the 'what if' method," he said. "What if he does get mad and accuses you of being a complainer? It's not going to hurt you that much."

What if? Think of the worst possible outcome. How bad can that be? Not half as bad as the gnawing, nagging feeling of being dealt with unfairly. Such a feeling may linger in your mind, and in Joan's case it would come back to haunt her whenever her grade average concerned her.

Your procrastination, like Joan's, may be doing something for you. It may be ministering to your sense of martyrdom—a sick sort of reaction. Joan finally did go to the professor in fear and trepidation only to discover that he was happy to look over her paper. It had been graded by a graduate student, she discovered. As Joan presented her apologies, he responded by complimenting her for demonstrating her assertiveness.

Ask yourself the "What if?" question. The answer may surprise you.

3. Am I acting responsibly or irresponsibly?

A responsible individual is a person of his word. When you belong to a group you make an unwritten contract to meet with the members at certain times. Some procrastinators are always "intending" to be at the meetings and if they do go, they always arrive late.

Jean Hopkins is like this. She is always late at every function she attends. When asked why, she always explains,

"There's no sense in getting there on time. Most of the other people are late. Why should I get into a panic and go racing around? I'm only going to have to wait for the others."

The answer is that whatever other people do has nothing to do with Jean's responsibility. Studies have shown that personal responsibility may be an important factor in mental health and when we procrastinate we may not only be gaining a reputation as a chronic laggard but we may be hurting our own mental health. Remind yourself that no matter how irresponsible others might be, you should do the right and responsible thing.

While we are procrastinating, life speeds by.
Seneca

4. When all else fails, try being honest.

William James, the famous psychologist, used to speak about the importance of confession. He referred to the practice as "exteriorizing our rottenness." Why don't we try using this practice in controlling the wretched practice of procrastination?

Suppose that you have been thinking about having your house painted. You know it really should be done, but every time you are half inclined to do it, a dozen reasons come to mind for leaving it a while longer. You know it's going to be a hassle.

Sit down with paper and pencil and write down every excuse that you offer when you put off doing something about the paint job. It doesn't matter how flimsy the excuses are, put them down on paper.

Now take an honest look at them. Do they make sense? Write at the bottom of your list, "These do not stand up. I'm going to get with it and do something." Maybe your postponed project isn't painting the house. Apply this to whatever it is that you've been putting off.

5. Use the appointment method.

List the things you have been putting off. Then take your calendar and write yourself a series of appointments. Put one of these things in for each day.

If you miss the event (through procrastination?), write it in again for another date. Don't let it get off your calendar. The annoyance of being continually faced with these responsibilities will become a motivator toward defeating your procrastinating tendencies.

6. You do not lack time.

The most common excuse of the procrastinator is, "I don't have enough time," or "I'm just too busy." It has been said that the most acceptable excuse for irresponsibility is busyness. Everybody is busy. The real question is, "What am I busy about?"

WE ALWAYS HAVE TIME FOR THE THINGS WE DO FIRST

The New Testament speaks about "redeeming the time" (Ephesians 5:16). The word came from the slave market where a man would hand over money to purchase a slave. We must be willing to purchase the time by deciding on the order of our priorities, focusing on the essentials, and trading off some of the time devoted to the less important things.

7. You are not surrendering your independence.

One outstanding educator has said, "No one is lazy except when accomplishing someone else's objectives." Temptations to procrastination often come from the feeling that someone else is deciding what needs to be done. We may get the feeling, "Why should I have to do that?" This attitude gives rise to resentment and one way we show resentment is by delaying action. We don't give an out-and-out refusal; we just never get to it.

Realize that you are playing games. The situation has nothing to do with independence and subservience. You are simply fostering a bad habit.

As you think alone and meditate about your time and how best to invest it, keep in mind that old man Procrastination stands within the shadow of everyone of us just waiting for his chance to spoil our success and lure us into wasting our time.

Paul Parker

8. Don't miss the "big event" by focusing on your own performance.

Without doubt, one of the most difficult vocations is that of being the pastor of a church. The job requires an individual of unusual resilience to withstand the rigors of an exacting task. Among the many frustrations of a minister's work is the task of getting the church worship service started on time.

I spend a lot of time with ministers in this situation and I have seen a side of this that is seldom open to the inspection of other mortals. The major culprit appears to be the minister of music. It seems as if this person feels it his responsibility to rehearse his choir "just one more time," while hundreds and in some instances thousands of people wait. I've watched those pastors sweating it out and I can almost see a stomach ulcer developing before my eyes. What can "just one more time" accomplish? Very little, it seems to me.

Procrastinators have only one person in mind—themselves. They fail to see the wider picture and live their lives in terms of their own immediate satisfaction. Learn to be a team player—don't miss, and in part spoil the big event by procrastinating and focusing on your own performance.

9. Be a pace-setter rather than a reactor.

For a three-year period I made a weekly six-hundred mile round trip on one of America's most famous trains. I have always enjoyed train travel, but in that three years I was completely disillusioned. That train was so frequently late that an on-time arrival or departure was an event to wonder at and talk about.

What a contrast this made with my experiences in Germany where I spent several summers traveling on the train. I was amazed when I received with my ticket a pamphlet listing the exact time of arrival and departure, with minutes specified, for every stop along the way. I was never late for a departure on that train system.

Some years ago an air carrier was jokingly referred to as "the largest unscheduled air carrier in the U.S." The procrastinator can all too easily build such a reputation and effectively sabotage his leadership potential.

This particular airline finally paid the penalty for its procrastination as its passengers moved to other airlines and it ultimately went bankrupt. It contrasts vividly with a printing establishment where, when I asked the representative,

"Are you sure you can get this job done on time?" he answered by pointing to a large sign which read NEVER A DISAPPOINTMENT. This is the attitude that builds a reputation and loyal clients.

10. Defeating procrastination may be a spiritual experience.

The Bible has a lot to say about time. President John Kennedy used to say his favorite passage from the Bible was the third chapter of the book of Ecclesiastes:

> To every thing there is a season, and a time to every purpose under the heaven:
> A time to be born, and a time to die;
> A time to plant, and a time to pluck up that which is planted;
> A time to kill, and a time to heal;
> A time to break down, and a time to build up;
> A time to weep, and a time to laugh. . . .
>
> Ecclesiastes 3:1–4

This passage makes it quite clear that we live in an ordered universe and the all-powerful God who presides over His creation has planned the events that impinge on our lives. Jesus referred to this when, following the resurrection, His disciples asked Him about the order of historical events. Jesus responded, "It is not for you to know the times or the seasons, which the Father hath put in his own power" (Acts 1:7). Because we do not know the precise timetable of what God is going to do we must be ready to fulfill our individual part of the bargain and not procrastinate but be on time.

The principle is applicable to the most fundamental of all spiritual experiences. As the Apostle Paul stood before the governor Felix and preached about righteousness, temperance, and judgment to come, Felix trembled, then responded, "Go thy way for this time; when I have a convenient season, I will call for thee" (Acts 24:25). The procrastinator had missed his moment of opportunity to experience salvation.

How different it was in the ministry of Jesus, who refused the blandishments of procrastination. He said, "I must work the works of him that sent me, while it is day; the night cometh, when no man can work" (John 9:4). The very best way to handle procrastination is to make it a spiritual issue and make a commitment to a life of accepting responsibilities as they come.

Don't Miss the Tide

In one of the great plots of history that helped to change the course of a nation, the plotters gathered to plan, one of them urging his coconspirators to take immediate action. He said:

There is a tide in the affairs of men,
Which taken at the flood, leads on to fortune;
Omitted, all the voyage of their life
Is bound in shallows and in miseries.
On such a full sea are we now afloat,
And we must take the current when it serves,
Or lose our ventures.

Julius Caesar
Act IV, Scene 3

Many of us are living our lives in shallows and miseries because we are procrastinators. We can find a multitude of reasons why we should not act at this time. There is also the easy rationalization that it is always important to take care not to make hasty decisions—the wisdom of suspending judgment until all the evidence is in. But it will never be in. The time is now. We must act.

Building an "On Time" Family

While traveling with a tour group in Europe, our bus was constantly delayed by a family power struggle. The mother, newly widowed, had great difficulty in managing her teenaged son, who was determined to show his independence by refusing to obey her, particularly when it came to departure times. He was always late and when he arrived, walked with a defiant, nonchalant air.

The result was that some thirty people sat cooling their heels until he wandered along. The concerned mother continually apologized. At last the group had enough. While waiting one day, at the driver's behest it was decided that commencing the next day the bus would go without the boy if he were not on time. The mother was asked to pass the news on to him.

The next morning at Florence, Italy, the departure time arrived and no Jimmy. With the mother's tearful agreement, the bus left minus the dilatory boy. Jimmy finally caught up with us two days later in Frankfurt, Germany. He was never late again.

Our families can become laboratories in which we can teach our children to be punctual.

1. Parents must commence by being on time themselves.
2. Elevate the concept of punctuality. Carefully enunciate the advantages that come to us when we are punctual.

3. Emphasize the social aspect. Present a situation like Jimmy's and evaluate an unpunctual person's effect on a number of people.

4. Establish a clear schedule for the family's day and try as much as possible to stick to it.

5. Focus on starting time. When something is to be done, make your plans allowing for a possible contingency. If something is to be done by the fifteenth, set a goal for the thirteenth. If the starting time is 8 P.M., plan to be there fifteen minutes ahead of time.

I once conducted church services with New Guinea natives who never came on time. So we played a game. If I wanted to start at 9:30 A.M., I announced the starting time as 9. They all turned up thirty minutes late and we started "on time." This might be all right with Stone Age people, but in a modern society we have a contract with others, and we should believe in the sanctity of contract. A way of doing this is to keep our word and be punctual.

Millions of people throughout the world go through life as failures because they have fallen prey to procrastination and decided to wait, always waiting for the time to be just right to start doing something they already know is good, worthwhile, and should be done at once. Don't delay. The time will never be just right. The only period of time we can act upon is right now. Start today, start right where you stand, and work with whatever tools you now have at your command.

Parker

6
Love Is Something You Do

"Do you, James Williams, take this woman, Jeanette Johnson, to be your lawfully wedded wife?"

"I do."

"And do you, Jeanette Johnson, take this man, James Williams, to be your lawfully wedded husband?"

"I do."

The phrase "I do" is so closely associated with marriage that a popular musical on the experience of marriage is called, "I Do! I Do!" If the expression were more true to the actual experience of marriage, it might more appropriately be "I Don't! I Don't!" or perhaps "I Won't! I Won't!"

Marriage is many things. It is an event, a ceremony that takes place at a given moment in time: "I was married on the ninth of December." It is an experience: "They were married and lived happily together for many years." It is a condition: "He is a married man." It can easily be thought of as a static condition.

This is not the view of this book. Our hypothesis is: MARRIAGE IS NOT A CONDITION. IT IS A WAY OF LIFE— AN ACTIVITY.

All too frequently this activity that we call marriage is built up as a feeling, an emotion to which is often given the name of love. When the feeling has subsided, as it surely will somewhere along the line, that may become the basis for terminating the relationship. The feeling has gone, and so has the relationship.

When faced with a situation like this I sometimes ask the question, "What is love?"

DECISIVE MOTIVATIONAL ACTION #6

Reconsider your ideas about love and see that at the most superficial level love is something you feel, at the marriage level it may be something you think, but at its best love is something you do. Consider the possibility of developing and rebuilding love by a series of actions.

There are many answers to this query. One way of looking at the love experience is to use the three Greek words *eros*, *philia*, and *agape*. Each involves some type of action. *Eros* is a movement of the emotions; it is something you feel. *Philia* is a movement of the mind; it is something you think. The third and highest level is *agape*, which is a movement of the total personality. We will consider each of these in turn.

Love Is Something You Feel

The most widely held idea of love is that it is preeminently an *eros*, emotional, romantic experience. Such a notion has led to some startling actions. Someone concluded that there are eight characteristics of an emotional, romantic love in its most intense form:

1. It is a dramatic and often unexpected experience that suddenly overtakes its victim.
2. Being "in love" may distort the judgment of the individual.
3. Love is a never-ending quest with the love object constantly evading the lover's grasp.
4. Being in love is preeminently an experience of the emotions.
5. The lover may be guilty of irrational behavior.
6. The experience may completely immobilize the "victim."
7. Preoccupation with the thoughts of the loved one could be described as obsessional.
8. There are frequently evidences of a well-formed delusional system in romantic love encounters.

While in this condition, the subject would not be capable of making rational decisions, least of all a lifelong commitment to another person and the propagation of a family.

Love Is Something You Think

The Greeks used the word *philia* to describe the relationship of two people who have a shared outlook on life. This has been called the friendship factor. The concept has validity and introduces ideas that are much more practical than the *eros*, romantic, emotional idea. There is something very appealing about the idea that a man's wife is his friend as well as his lover.

Philia or friendship love differs from romantic love in a number of ways:

- Romantic lovers are looking at each other. *Philia* lovers are side by side looking in the same direction.
- Romantic lovers idealize their love object. *Philia* lovers recognize their friend's faults and still accept them "warts and all."
- Romantic lovers wittingly or unwittingly are drawn by physical attractiveness. *Philia* lovers are drawn together by a mental affinity.
- Romantic lovers want to be by themselves. *Philia* lovers want to increase their circle of friends.

Shared interests and a similar outlook on life are of great moment in building a solid man-woman relationship. Two people have a shared interest, a common outlook on life. The romantic, sexual, emotional will fluctuate in intensity but the common intellectual interest will continue on. Looking at the *philia* element in marriage, a spouse is seen as a companion and a friend. *Philia* love gives stability to a relationship that is lacking at the *eros* or emotional level. It is an action love, action at the intellectual level, and paves the way for consideration of the third and most important level.

Love Is Something You Do

The great, rich, Christian word for love is the Greek word *agape*. It is used to describe God's love for men and women and then the love that Christians should have for each other.

The idea of doing, of giving, is predominant in this love. Paul sets it forth in all its glory in 1 Corinthians 13, where the constant refrain is of an altruistic love:

This love of which I speak is slow to lose patience—it looks for a way of being constructive. It is not possessive: it is neither anxious to impress nor does it cherish inflated ideas of its own importance. Love has good manners and does not pursue selfish advantage. It is not touchy. It does not keep account of evil or gloat over the wickedness of other people.
1 Corinthians 13:4, 5 PHILLIPS

Paul's exposition stands like a towering mountain in a desert wasteland, when compared with the literature of antiquity on the subject of love. The main difference is the emphasis on action, altruistic action.

Agape love is particularly applicable to home and family life and has significance for husbands and wives. A man comes in for counseling, saying that he is contemplating divorce because he no longer loves his wife. By this statement he generally means he doesn't feel the same way toward her as he did formerly, or possibly he doesn't think the same way as she does. "I have outgrown her intellectually," he says.

In each of these situations he is saying either, "Love is something I feel" or "Love is something I think." The third and all-important idea is the action imperative, that love is something you do. The answer to the statement, "I do not love my wife," would be, "Can you not do something for her?"

Utilizing Action-love to Repair a Relationship

A rift in the relationship of husband and wife can have devastating effects on a family and lead to its dismemberment. As we have already noted, this situation may come to pass because of the emphasis on romantic love. If falling in love is the basis of marriage, runs the argument, then falling out of love means there is no reason to sustain the marriage, so divorce is the answer.

The Bible tells us about another way. A passage in the book of Revelation, although addressed to a church, lays down three principles that can be tremendously effective in repairing a husband-wife relationship, by utilizing the love concept. The statement is, "Think about those times of your first love . . . and turn back . . . again and work as you did before" (Revelation 2:5 TLB).

Here is the program:

1. Remember. "Think about your first love."

Spend some time thinking about the experiences that went into the making of this relationship. Recollect your dating days, your happy experiences together, your marriage, your honeymoon, the birth of a child, and the multitude of experiences that have gone into the making of the years you have invested in this relationship.

Recall the Law of Pre- and Postmarital Perceptions: "Before marriage the loved one's virtues are perceived and faults overlooked. Following marriage, faults are magnified and virtues overlooked."

In consideration of this law, forget the negative things you tend to exaggerate, and face the possibility that you may in reality be trying to evade responsibility. Remember, too, that the present object of your affections has probably been fantasized in your mind, and will probably look quite different if that relationship ceased to be illicit, and were legitimatized. Consider the good things about the relationship you may be ending. Remember.

2. Turn Back—"turn back again."

Be willing to turn your back on this present attraction. Give yourself a chunk of time within which you will have breathing space and be able to make a sensible decision. Make sure that you are not rushing into a situation and taking an action you may live to regret. Decide that above everything else you are going to deliberately focus on the possibilities and potentialities that are dormant within your present relationship.

3. Take Action—"work as you did before."

Love and hate have a strange ambivalence in human personality. Any marriage counselor can tell of the strange paradox of two people who at one time spent their moments together looking into each other's eyes, touching fingers, whispering sweet nothings, who now in a deteriorated relationship see everything as negative and every expression as hostile in their spouse. Margaret Swan was the personification of this strange phenomenon.

An attractive, thirty-five-year-old woman, Margaret sat talking with Jim Stephens, attorney at law, and was obviously seething with bitterness. "That dirty rat. He was nothing. I made him—my money, my daddy's influence. Now I discover that all this time he has been involved in an affair with Jean, who I thought was my best friend. I am certainly going to divorce him, but I want to make him pay, really pay."

Margaret pressed home her point with the attorney, "Now counselor, I need your help. I know you've had your own problems with Nelson. Will you help me not only get a divorce but also make him pay for what he's done to me?"

Jim Stephens finally laid out the plan that would suit them both. He said, "You're an attractive woman, Margaret. If Nelson has any sense he would have realized this. It's only an infatuation with this other woman, and it probably happened because you had so many interests and did not pay attention to him, leaving him with time on his hands.

"Here is our plan. You really go after him—woo him until you win him back. Make him fall madly in love with you again; and when you have him eating out of your hand, drop him like a hot coal, divorce him, then watch him suffer."

Margaret went to work with might and main and brought her not inconsiderable powers to bear on Nelson. Three months later she returned to her attorney's office to report her success. She had not only outwitted her rival but Nelson was her virtual slave.

Attorney Stephens smiled in personal satisfaction at the news of the way she had pulled off his plan. "Well, let's get on with it. Let's file for the divorce," he urged.

"File for divorce?" Margaret responded. "No way. I've really fallen in love with Nelson all over again."

Margaret Swan, by her action plan, had rebuilt a love for this man whom she thought she hated. *Agape* love, a love that acts, has a tremendous potential for reaching out and influencing people. Within a family this self-giving, acting love is one indispensable element that makes a family into what God wants it to be.

In the male-female relationships that ultimately culminate in marriage, action in the love experience involves an important sequence of the levels of love. *Eros* or romantic love may move the emotions, spark an interest, and mark the beginning of an authentic relationship, but it is only a beginning. *Philia* or intellectual love builds a basis apart from the emotional and provides the companionship and friendship which make for a long-lasting relationship. But it is the *agape,* giving, acting love that will be the capstone of the love experience.

LOVE'S FLOWER PETALS NEVER FALL

7

Your Mind Is a Muscle

 No better example of physical movement and the part it plays in individual, national, and international life could be found than in that great contest of athletic prowess, the Olympic Games. But though the Games are greatly respected and prized as the pinnacle of athletic competition, they have become a promoter's nightmare and have too often left the sponsoring nation with financial problems.

To coin a phrase, venue doesn't mean revenue.

Although countries have previously contended with each other for the privilege of hosting the Games, such was not the case in 1984. Only one city applied for the Games—Los Angeles. Many of the inhabitants of the "City of Angels" were not exactly ecstatic about the privilege that was to be theirs when Los Angeles was awarded the Games. The financial liabilities likely to accrue to the taxpayers worried them. This led the organizing committee to reach a decision to be more considerate of a city's purse in setting up the Games.

Early on, because of the expense involved, it was decided that it was inadvisable to build an Olympic village. In answer to the criticism that this would defeat the object of drawing the contestants close to each other, the chairman of the committee responded, "We invented the concept of the Olympic Village in 1932—now we are disinventing it."

DECISIVE MOTIVATIONAL ACTION #7

Realize that the action principle has an application to your intellectual capacity. One creditable assumption is that your mind is like a muscle that needs exercise; movement of the body may generate ideas.

To head up the organization of the 1984 Games, the committee chose Peter Ueberroth, a highly-successful businessman known for his "enlightened stinginess." Ueberroth has an interest in sports and once made an unsuccessful tryout for the U.S. Olympic water polo team. But he did not consider himself the likely organizer of a great city as host of the Games. When first offered the position, he said he was not interested. But he later allowed himself to be persuaded and left his dynamic First Travel Corporation in other hands. Finally, he sold the enterprise.

The committee decided that the organization of the Games would reflect the American free enterprise system. By involving American business in the venture, one observer noted, "This man Ueberroth and his team are going to make money for the city of Los Angeles, for the Olympics, and for just about everybody else, including the sponsors." And that's exactly what happened. Ueberroth's ability in organizing was demonstrated to the organizing committee when the Los Angeles Games turned a handsome profit, and to the sports world when he was selected as the new baseball commissioner and named *Time* magazine's "Man of the Year."

This remarkable personality grew up in a home where another and ultimately more important type of athletics was regular fare. *Time* quoted him as saying of his father, "We would discuss world issues at dinner. Or he would toss riddles out on the table. It was mental gymnastics."

His father would be pleased to see his son perpetuated the practice of mental gymnastics, not only in his home but also in the offices of the Los Angeles Olympic Organizing Committee. His staffers referred to these sessions as "Peter Tests." This organizational coach tested his staff members by calling upon them to name the president of the International Olympic Committee, the site of the 1984 Winter Games, the capital of Yugoslavia, or ten foreign cities of more than one million population whose names start with the letter M.

In keeping with his father's concept of mental gymnastics, and in the mystique of the Olympic Games, Ueberroth states his conviction:

YOUR MIND IS LIKE A MUSCLE—YOU MUST EXERCISE IT

The notion of the mind being like a muscle is not original and has been propagated for many years. Many of the practices of educators, particularly in the area of rote learning, have been built on a basis similar to this.

If the analogy has any validity it will remind us that muscle-building is a demanding business. It involves hours of repetition and if practice is missed the muscle begins to deteriorate at a pretty fast clip. The major opportunity for exercising the mind lies in the area of reading. There the wisdom of the ages has been recorded and preserved for us. With tremendous numbers of new books being published every year, the literature on the shelves of our libraries provides a continuing challenge to the individual who would be literate.

The way you exercise your mind might affect the way you move in your interpersonal relationships. A doctoral student in a psychology program undertook a project of investigating what factors are brought into play in improving an individual's self-image. He divided his subjects into three groups: one, a therapy group, a second in which therapy was combined with a specific reading program, and a third which concentrated on the reading program alone.

Each of these participants was tested about his or her self-concept before and after the experience. The second group, involved both with therapy and reading, showed the greatest improvement. The reading group showed the second greatest improvement, while those who experienced only therapy indicated the least advance.

The student concluded after this research that a carefully-designed reading program has tremendous potential in helping people develop a healthy concept of themselves.

But will people move their muscle minds?

Remembering the admonition of Bacon that "reading maketh a full man," I am frequently shocked at how little mental muscle-building, in the form of reading, is done. Being

involved in the writing and selling of books I am horrified by
the number of times people standing by the book display at a
conference will comment, "You know, I never read a book."
One researcher claims that less than 25 percent of the population ever sit down to seriously read a book.

There may be a glimmer of hope. Shocked by reports of
low academic achievement and poor performance in basic
skills such as reading and math, some school systems are
making an effort to remedy the situation. These imaginative
educators are transferring some of the glamour of the athletic field to the arena of academics.

Schools in various parts of the country have inaugurated a
series of Academic Olympics and report a developing student interest. Whereas in the past, coveted "letters" were
given to the athletes, now some schools are awarding letters
in English, math, and other academic areas. It may be that
the concept of the "muscle mind" has something to com-
mend it.

Areas in which we should exercise our muscle minds by
reading books include the following:

- Read good history books, remembering that they who fail
  to learn the lessons of history are destined to repeat its
  mistakes.
- Take time with the biography of some of the really greats;
  enter into the experiences of others.
- Learn to experience the joy of being lost in a really good
  book.
- Give your attention to the self-help and motivational
  books.
- Spend some time with good Christian literature, missionary biography, church history.
- Study the Bible. It is the greatest book of all. Remember
  the exhortation, "give attention to reading."

THE MUSCLES ARE PREEMINENTLY THE TEACHERS AND EDUCATORS OF THE BRAIN

Action and learning go hand in hand. We have long known that a quiescent student doesn't learn very much. The student must at least be *mentally* active if he is to learn, but it may be that *physical* activity is also an important part of the process.

The conscientious teacher will discover that devising appropriate activities for his or her student will test the student's ingenuity. The way the teacher involves the student in activity may be the measure of his or her teaching skill.

One expert in the realm of the mind, psychiatrist Abraham Low, has discovered that the way to affect the mind might well be by moving the body. His perceptive book, *Mental Health Through Will-Training,* as the title implies, sets out an action program. This psychiatrist states his premise as, "The muscles are preeminently the teachers and the educators of the brain." From this follows a program for ex-mental hospital patients that majors on action. A characteristic statement to a participant in the program is, "Move your muscles."

Which Came First?

We are immediately confronted with the question concerning the way people learn. One way to outline the learning process is:

mastering material → understanding → changed behavior
The experience of teachers with this content approach has not been very encouraging. Students have memorized material and regurgitated it on demand, but it has never been translated into behavior.

We must consider another possibility which may be para-digmed:

practice new behavior → satisfaction → understanding

Affirmation for this point of view comes from an unusual source. In the economic miracle of modern Japan, news has come about one of the driving forces—seventy-seven-year-old industrialist Toshiwo Doko, a genius at breathing new life into faltering enterprises. Described as a man of action, he has demonstrated the action premise. Doko's favorite saying is, "Act instead of thinking it over. Only action produces ideas."

Establishing a Family Learning Center

In one type of group therapy we ask people to think back on their childhood days and answer the question, "What was the warmest room in the house?" Almost invariably they answered that it was the kitchen, the place where the meals were prepared and eaten and where the family gathered to discuss the affairs of the day. How about establishing a family forum so the family members can exercise their muscle minds?

A study of communal enterprises by Rosabeth Kanter indicated that all of the successful groups had regular group meetings. If we can persuade parents and children to use the mealtime gathering—usually the evening meal—for a family forum, it will have a double value as a means of learning and also strengthening the family as a unit.

Guidelines for using the family forum will include the following:

1. Have all the members of the family assemble and eat their meal at the same time.

2. Share the table-waiting duties. Don't let mother be the unpaid waitress.

3. Turn off the television. It is impossible to carry on an intelligent conversation while the TV demands both eyes and ears.

4. Utilize the time as a celebration. Remember the birthdays of family members, and the great religious and patriotic occasions as well.

5. Ask family members to report on their day. Did anybody hear a joke, a funny story, or a riddle he would like to share?

6. Introduce a subject for discussion and give each member a chance to have his say. Try to reach a conclusion and make a summary of the pros and cons.

7. Try the Ueberroth technique: "We would discuss world issues at dinner. Or father would toss out riddles on the table. It was mental gymnastics."

8. At the conclusion of the meal, let all the family members work at cleaning up. It can be fun, and an activity that has learning potentialities.

Let Your Fingers Do the Thinking

Among creative people, writers stand high, for theirs is a field in which this peculiar breed of people must regularly produce in what has been called the loneliest of all activities: writing. The writer's major problem is to get an idea out of his head and transfer it to some recorded written form.

The means of transferring these ideas is constantly changing. Our predecessors drew their ideas on the walls of a cave or a primitive building, chiseled them out on stone, marked them on leather, inscribed them on papyrus or, later, wrote on paper. In modern times, the writer used a pen or pencil, or a typewriter, a dictating machine, or computer.

If he is using either a typewriter, a pen or a word processor he is engaging in what has been called finger-tip thinking. The telephone company has long tried to boost the use of its Yellow Pages with the slogan, "Let your fingers do the walking." As authors have taken to pen, typewriter, and computer, they have turned to the direction of "Let your fingers do the talking." Now we have the idea of "Let your fingers do your thinking." Finger-tip thinking expresses the idea that finger movement may be a factor in triggering the brain's creative activity.

"The Work of Thy Fingers"

The place of fingers in creativity is seen in many of the arts, such as needlepoint, sculpture, music, and painting, and almost any type of work involving manual activity.

A report on the injuries to Americans in the workplace indicated that fingers are so highly prized and need such care that they accounted for about 25 percent of the visits of workers to the emergency room, and cost about $83.3 million in 1982. In the therapy sometimes used with children called finger painting, the digit seems to have some particular therapeutic value.

The Bible speaks of fingers as very special things. In God's creative work, the psalmist says, "When I consider thy heavens, the work of thy fingers . . ." (Psalms 8:3). When reference is made to the most influential statement of ethical principle ever made—the giving of the Ten Commandments—Moses recorded that the Commandments were inscribed on tables of stone, ". . . written with the finger of

God" (Exodus 31:18). The preparation of the Levitical offerings, so integral a part of Israel's worship, is explained with sixteen specific references to the "fingers" of the priests. In the book of Proverbs the wicked person is said to be teaching with his fingers (see Proverbs 6:13), and when Jesus wanted to convey a very delicate and special message He leaned over and wrote with His finger on the ground (see John 8:6).

The fingers are also seen to be of significance in that the Lord commanded the people to tie His words "on their fingers," a statement which carries the implication that the Word of God has some special application to the activity of the fingers. Each of these statements carries the implication that the fingers are particularly important. Each lays a heavy stress on the act of writing as a communication technique involving the use of the fingers.

The Ease of Writing

One writer claims that writing is always easy, except on three occasions: when you're getting started, when you've got to keep going, and when you are trying to finish.

The first of these, getting started, is the most difficult and important, for if there is no starting then there is certainly no finishing, in fact nothing at all.

I once talked with the author of a series of very popular books on electronics. His books sold widely in two countries, maybe more, and he seemed to have it made. Trying to take advantage of my opportunity to learn something from a master of the writer's craft I asked, "How do you start your work day?"

He smiled at me and replied, "How do I get started? With great difficulty. I eat a leisurely breakfast and then I read the paper. I go out into the yard and examine the flowers, call a couple of friends—in other words, I do anything I can to avoid starting work."

Finger-tip Thinking

This honest man had pinpointed the major problem in all creative work. It is a matter of getting started, in a word: moving. One way of doing this is to sit down and just write whatever comes to mind and has some sort of relationship to the subject under consideration.

The very process of writing will generate ideas. This is particularly so in using a word processor where the words almost magically appear on a screen in front of the writer in response to the movement of his fingers on the keys.

REACH OUT AND GRAB THE FABRIC OF YOUR OWN CONSCIOUSNESS WITH ALL YOUR TEN FINGERS. SHAKE THE TRUTH WITHIN YOU UNTIL IT FLAMES WITH REALITY

It has been said that the writing process is a direct path from the mind to the page. The fingers are the mechanical means used in facilitating this process.

What is the best way to do this? Action.

As Rod Serling says it, "The new writer should observe, listen, look . . . and then write. Nothing begets better writing than the simple process of writing."

Sprinting, Striding, and Strolling

Once again, not just any action will do, but three particular types of action which vary all the way from speed to deliberation. These actions may be categorized as the sprint, the stride, and the stroll.

Sprinting involves writing as rapidly as you can without giving too much attention to the organization and format of your material. If you happen to be using a word processor you can enjoy the added consolation of knowing that you can easily reorganize your material later. The sheer sensation of getting it down quickly and the sense of achievement can often stimulate the thought processes.

Striding is the slower pace into which you begin to lapse. It would not be possible to sprint on for long periods of time, any more than the runner could keep up his hundred-yard-dash pace for a mile. In this stage you are thinking more of the logic of what you are writing and the way in which it is going to move.

Strolling is the stage of moving backwards and forwards, of pausing to take a critical look at and reconsider what you have been writing. The secret of writing is *rewriting*. Do some of it over again. Massage it by adding a word, changing a hackneyed statement, dividing an overlong paragraph, shortening a sentence. Put it aside and then go over it again. What seemed like a purple passage in the sprint stage may look altogether different in this third stage.

Incubation

The human mind is a wonder to behold, and one of the most interesting aspects is its creative function. It does not stay still, but is constantly on the move and once it begins to grapple with ideas it often continues on without any effort of the will. This activity is frequently seen as the function of the unconscious portion of the mind and is sometimes referred to as incubation. In much the same way as the egg is placed in the incubator and develops until a chicken is hatched, so the idea or concept grows and develops.

One poet likened the process to dropping a letter into the mailbox and leaving it there only to return and discover the ideas had expanded and developed. John Dewey, the eminent philosopher, used to tell his students about the way they could use these unconscious powers as ideas incubated and developed.

However, the philosopher had a word of warning to those who thought their unconscious might just take over and do all the work: "But this bringing forth of inventions, solutions, and discoveries rarely occurs except to a mind that has previously steeped itself consciously in material relating to its question, and has turned the matters over and over, weighing pros and cons."

Dewey was reminding us that creativity is action. No action, no creativity. Once in motion, the mind very naturally moves on its way, continuing to gain creative momentum. But before it does, the individual must work and act, and once having applied himself to the matter with vigor he discovers he has an ally as the creative unconscious takes over.

Do you want to learn to write?

- The only way to learn to write is to write. Undertake some type of writing assignment.
- Start by writing the simple courtesy notes that will help you build relationships as well as your communications skills.
- Learn to type. It will pay off in many ways and you will learn interactive skills that can facilitate your creativity.
- There is only one surefire formula for writers—the application of the seat of the pants to the seat of the chair.
- One caveat to the above: It is all in vain unless moving fingers are applied to the keyboard.

- All creative activity requires *action*—either intellectual or physical—and very frequently the physical stimulates the intellectual.
- Try some finger-tip thinking. Take your pencil or pen in hand, sit at your typewriter or word processor, and try some sprinting, then move to striding and strolling.
- The existence of the Sabbath day reminds us that creativity requires such labor that after the supreme productive work, the Creator had to rest.

Your fingerprints may indicate your uniqueness, but your finger movements are creativity-generators: let your fingers do the thinking.

Preserving Family Roots

Writing skills may be one of the most valuable assets your family members can have. Why not do something to develop them?

How about commencing a project on the family history? Outside our back door in the cement patio are the footprints of Larry, Nancy, and Betsy. They were made twenty-five years ago. I often wish they could come back and put their feet in the same spot today, but they can't; they live somewhere else in another part of the country.

Every family has a story to tell and it needs a storyteller. Let every member of the family be that storyteller. Encourage your children to write little pieces about their experiences and read them during family forum time. Keep them carefully.

Establish a family history depository. It can be as simple as a shoe box or elaborate as a filing cabinet with manila folders.

Encourage your children to get into the habit of writing

thank you notes. They will learn the skill of building relationships and at the same time take some steps in developing writing skills.

Do you have a deaf friend? There's a possibility your children might like to learn sign language. It generally fascinates children, helps them to learn the importance of fingers and how they can be an instrument for communication, and gives them an opportunity to render a very real service.

Staying One Play Ahead

Professional football coaches come in a wide variety. Their difficult task includes selecting, training, and giving leadership to a team of athletes who are often as temperamental and sensitive as a group of opera stars. They have an obligation both to the owners and the fans who expect them to win every game they play.

The leadership styles among coaches are highly individualistic. The fabled Vince Lombardi exercised such an iron control over his players that one of them once stated, "He treats us all the same; like dogs." John Madden used the sideline of the football field as a stage upon which to demonstrate his not inconsiderable dramatic abilities. This thespian of the sideline acted out emotions worthy of a Laurence Olivier, shouting, protesting, swooning, and appearing in grave danger of apoplexy. Madden seemed to expend much more energy on his sideline dramatics than did his players on the field.

Amid this scene of prima donna coaches stands another individual, Tom Landry. A man of strong Christian convictions—who once stated his loyalties were to God, family, and football, in that order—he presents an entirely different image. Landry is known to many as the Great Stone Face. One commentator noted that Landry's expression during a game vacillates from, "Where am I?" to "Did something happen?"

Landry's stoic countenance, preoccupation with the game plan on his clipboard, and use of the computer lead his critics to sneer at "computerized football." Nevertheless he has had the last laugh and stands as professional football's winningest active coach. Of him the Green Bay Packers' Bart Starr said, "What Tom Landry has accomplished over the years is nothing short of remarkable. He has won consistently, and he has won with class."

He is an actionist of a different type.

Goals Initiate Actions

I once visited a home where the family kept a pet kangaroo. The animal had been rescued after its mother was killed by a hunter, and these people had carefully reared the animal until it was large enough to manage for itself. They then faced a problem of another type. Following the instincts of its ancestry, the animal would periodically rush up and down the yard, absolutely decimating the family's beautiful vegetable and flower gardens. This is the style of some actionists who rush madly into the fray without thought or consideration.

Landry represents action of another type. Often described as "one of football's greatest technical innovators," he might properly be called a "cerebral coach." When chided for not displaying more emotion, Landry explained the reason. "I think you have to train yourself to concentrate, and that's what I am doing on the sidelines during the game. I don't see the game the way the fans do. I'm one play ahead all the time. While the team is running one play, I'm looking ahead, planning the next one. I suppose that's why I don't react to a play the way the fans do."[10]

In many ways Landry represents the action premise advocated in this book. Not concerned about the stimulus effect of his personality, Landry is using his muscle mind to produce a football team of players who win consistently in a very physical game. He has demonstrated that the muscular mind is frequently more important than the muscular body. No helter-skelter rushing around like the kangaroo, destroying much of the valuable development which is the result of so much arduous labor, but an activity that is goal-oriented and purposeful.

"While the team is running one play, I'm looking ahead, planning the next one."

Planning and preparing are integral parts of an action program. They may, in fact, provide many of the satisfactions that one gains from an action program. Sometimes anticipation is greater than realization. However, to see the carefully-planned action unfolding gives a peculiar sense of satisfaction.

From the unlikely field of professional football we are introduced to the possibility of action, not unpremeditated, but the result of careful planning.

Winston Churchill was a remarkably fine writer, but even he had his difficult moments. He experienced the monotony and even boredom that frequently accompanies this creative activity. On one occasion he described the process of writing.

It is an adventure. To begin with it is a toy and an amusement. Then it becomes a mistress, then it becomes a master, then it becomes a tyrant. The last phase is that just as you

are about to be reconciled to your servitude, you kill the
monster and fling him to the public.

The momentum that made the writing become a monster
and a tyrant is part of the creativity cycle that develops as
the mind grapples with an idea and discerns its ramifica-
tions. The "monster" would never have been killed and
thrown to the public if there had not been the original adventure. It took an action to get it under way.

One author described a little ceremony he and his secretary went through as they made their way to the post office
and mailed off the manuscript. "What a sweet relief it was!"
I then inquired as to his next action and to my amazement
he replied that as soon as he returned to his office he sat
down and planned his next writing project. Like Landry he
was looking ahead to the next play in the game.

In the creative process, momentum is the name of the
game. Once the juices are running it is easy to keep on. The
world of television gives us excellent examples of this. A
successful TV series has a spin-off in which one segment of
the show develops a new life of its own. One thing grows out
of the other. It is a product of movement-momentum. One
book grows out of another.

Goals and objectives must forever be before us. Alexander
of Macedon grew up in a Greek state where soldiering skills
were highly prized. As he played with other young Greeks
the news would periodically come of his father Philip's victories. On one such occasion he turned to his playmates and
lamented, "My father is going to win all the battles before I
grow up." Of course, history shows that he won quite a few
victories himself. This forward-looking prince reaped the reward of his attitude when he became the renowned
Alexander the Great.

I Will Do It Better Next Time

There are history books and there are history books. Some of them are so dull that they send the reader off to sleep in a hurry. Then there are the other type which keep the reader sitting on the edge of his chair in a state of suspense seeking to discover what will happen next. One that falls into this latter category is Thomas Carlyle's *The French Revolution*. Charles Dickens frankly acknowledged that he was indebted to this volume for the background of his *Tale of Two Cities*.

At the time of its writing, Carlyle sent the completed first volume to the philosopher, John Stuart Mill, who had requested it. Mill's maid, seeking some kindling for lighting the fire, had picked up the manuscript on the table and, with the exception of four pages, burned it all. It was a disaster for Carlyle, but he tried to keep his frustration and disappointment from Mill, whom he thought had been careless with the manuscript.

After Mill's departure from the house, Carlyle sat down and wrote in his diary that he had sharp pains as if something were cutting him around the heart. That night he was plagued with horrible nightmares of his dead mother and sister. But the following day he wrote that he felt like a schoolboy who had laboriously written his copy and the Master (he carefully spelled the word with a capital M) had said, "No, boy, you must go and write it better."

Carlyle stayed one play ahead. He wrote a letter of comfort to Mill telling the philosopher that he had new and better paper for the rewriting, repeating the words he had uttered when Mill first broke the news of the tragic incident—*"I will write it better next time."*

The family tragedy that so injured Thomas Carlyle might be analogous to some of the misfortunes that befall us in family life. This is the place where we are most vulnerable, as the ones we love so much may cause us pain and distress by their thoughtless attitudes. Like Carlyle, we must learn to accept the situation as a learning experience and decide how we will do it better "next time." Whatever misfortunes befall the actionist family they hold their heads high and learn to stay one play ahead. One of the ways they do this is by setting family goals and objectives.

Family Goals

My wife and I have as one of our objectives physical fitness and improved health. To gain this objective we maintain a program of regular exercise, including walking. Near our home, in a beautiful, wooded area, is a delightful trail with distance markers; it provided an excellent setting for our objective of walking three miles in forty-five minutes at least five mornings a week.

Once we reached our objective speed of fifteen-minute miles, we seemed to get stuck. Then we purchased a stopwatch and timed the various segments of our walk; with shortened objectives for each segment our pace immediately increased. First, the long-range objective and then the more immediate objectives.

The achievers in life not only set up goals but also commit them to paper. People who write down their goals generally attain them. Let us set up goals for our family, and one good way of doing this is by beginning with four questions:

1. What are the long-range goals for our family? What do we want to achieve for our family unit? For father ... mother ... and each of the children?

2. What do individual family members—father, mother, children—want to achieve in the next three years?

3. Think of the worst possible scenario. Supposing a catastrophe befell you in a year's time. What would you like the family to have been doing during that period?

4. How about three months' time? What do you want the family to accomplish?

Establish the A-B-C priority system. In any list of activities, the items will never all be of equal value; some will be of greater value than others. Place the letter A alongside those of high value, B alongside those of medium value, and C alongside those of low value.

Write it all out on a piece of paper. Commence with lifetime goals and then work your way down to your goals for three months. Now, having planned your actions, go to it and act your plans. With these goals set out you will be ready to stay one play ahead in the game of life.

8
The Present Controls the Past

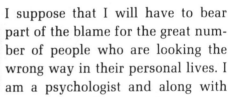I suppose that I will have to bear part of the blame for the great number of people who are looking the wrong way in their personal lives. I am a psychologist and along with the members of my profession I have spent much time telling people the importance of the early years of life. In all honesty our major objective has been to motivate the parents, teachers, and caretakers of children to do their best to give their charges the very best start in life.

Alas for our intentions. People had heard other messages from students of the human psyche like Sigmund Freud. He, too, emphasized the significance of the early years, but with a far more questionable purpose and has been quoted as saying that the experiences of the first few years of life determine what the rest of life is to be.

This attitude has been called *determinism*, defined as the teaching that "... an event is completely explicable in terms of its antecedents. Applied to human actions it holds that given complete knowledge of conditions, one would have complete knowledge of precisely how a person will—indeed *must*—act."

So came a psychological determinism which could be summed up in the statement, "The drama of life is but a repetition of the plot of infancy." This encouraged an attitude of fatalism which said in effect, "I got a raw deal with my lousy childhood; too bad I can't do anything about it."

The Paralysis of Analysis

The rather strange aspect of the work of Sigmund Freud and the dynamic psychologists is that their activities were carried on in the field of psychotherapy. Excursions into their clients' past were aimed at discovering the traumatic events of the past that might be affecting their adjustment to life in the present. It was somewhat ironic that many of their clients undergoing analysis showed no improvement.

DECISIVE MOTIVATIONAL ACTION #8

Face the tired old idea that the past makes us what we are, and realize that the present may affect the past much more than the past affects the present. Learn anew the danger of moving in the wrong direction.

One reason for this situation might well have been that the therapist had built such an elaborate case, proving that events of early days had caused the problem, that no way of escape now appeared to the client.

A characteristic comment of a client after many hours were spent probing into the past to discover the likely causes of neurotic maladaptive behavior, was, "Now that I know what it was that caused me to be like this, what am I going to do about it?" The trouble is that many therapists have not spent much time considering what the client should do.

All too frequently, the time and labor spent on looking back into the events of earlier years has led to a "paralysis of analysis," leaving the client bogged down in a morass of the past.

THE PRESENT MAY AFFECT THE PAST MUCH MORE THAN THE PAST AFFECTS THE PRESENT

Fortunately, other psychologists raised their voices in protest against this attitude. One of these stated the situation: "It may be that the present affects the past much more than the past affects the present." People look back selectively and have a tendency to recall earlier experiences which they think offer an explanation for what is happening at this moment. In this way the present affects the past.

Forget what happened in childhood or any earlier period of life; we have to live in the present and take the attitude of the Apostle Paul who said, "... forgetting those things which are behind, and reaching forth unto those things which are before, I press toward the mark ..." (Philippians 3:13,14).

Have a Fickle Love Affair with the Past

If anyone has justification for looking back to the past, it would surely be the distinguished 87-year-old George Burns, entertainer par excellence. Burns points out that he has no desire to live in the past. He claims he doesn't spend his time looking at scrapbooks of his past glories or read his past reviews. "They were painful enough to read the first time," he quips.

Burns completely rejects the notion that life begins at forty. He says it begins every morning when you wake up, and he claims he falls in love with what he is doing today. The things that he did yesterday were the things he loved then, but the romance is over. He adds, "I'm very fickle."

Burns himself remains the living example of his own philosophy. He readily admits that in his younger days much of his success was due to his wife Gracie. He was more a foil for her wit. Now he stands in his own right and does not intend to look back. He expresses his sympathy for people who live in the past, and adds:

YOU CAN'T KEEP LOOKING IN THE REARVIEW MIRROR—UNLESS YOU ENJOY HAVING A STIFF NECK!

Few cities of the world could ever outdo Salzburg as a scenic, historical, and preeminently musical attraction. For most Americans, Salzburg means not only Mozart and the classics, but "The Sound of Music." My wife and I had the privilege not only of being entertained in a home close by the Von Trapp family residence, but also traveling around the area where the movie was filmed.

The climax came when we took a trip by cable car to the Untersberg, 6,000 feet above Salzburg, where the movie producers filmed the famous escape scene of "The Sound of Music." The Von Trapp family had eluded Nazi surveillance at the music festival and climbed over the mountain on their way to Switzerland and freedom. When Salzburgers view this climactic scene they smile because the actual route over the Untersberg would have led the party back into Nazi Germany rather than to Switzerland. They were going in the wrong direction.

This is about the way it is in all of life. Movement should be the basic principle of life, but not just movement for its own sake. Moving backward can mean loss of freedom and a return to a fettered existence. Climb every mountain, but make sure you are headed in the right direction! No turning back, no turning back.

Year Zero

Time magazine ran an article concerning an Italian businessman who had been highly successful in his marketing enterprises. Although his high-powered program had achieved so much he was not about to sit back and take it easy. Making his plans for a new push for increased business in the USA, he stated his philosophy, "For me, this is year zero. Everything we've done before was nothing. Now we take off."

Year Zero. For him who would accomplish something of significance, both the failures and the triumphs of yesterday are over and done; this very moment is a fresh start.

It is true that we should not minimize the achievements of the past. I agree with the philosophy of the man who said, "It is better to be a 'has been' than a 'never was.' " But it is better still to see the present situation as Year Zero and be a forward-looker to the possibilities of tomorrow.

Lookers-Back Are Imprisoned by a Negative Emotion

June Todd's name is "failed marriage." She is so bitter about the husband who divorced her that all her energies are diverted to her hostility to him.

Harry Wymer's name might well be "passed over." He missed the promotion that he thought was rightly his and resents every aspect of the company he works with.

Betty Howard could be called "ungrateful kid." Her son upon whom she lavished her love and slender means has gone off and she never hears from him. So she bores her friends and neighbors with her laments of the gross ingratitude of offspring.

All of these and many others have a legitimate basis for their complaints. The trouble is that they are hurting the wrong people—friends, relatives, and neighbors who are sick to death of hearing their complaints. But primarily, they are damaging themselves.

Destroy the Tools of Servitude to the Past

The Dickens character Manette was a prisoner of the past. A highly successful Parisian physician, he had been wrongfully imprisoned in the notorious Bastille where long years of solitary confinement brought a complete loss of personal identity. In prison his sole interest lay in making shoes; instead of a name, he responded to a number—"One Hundred Five North Tower." This unfortunate man was released and allowed to return to his medical practice but he was so imprisoned by the past that when under tension, he would periodically become "One Hundred Five North Tower."

People are just as surely imprisoned today. We don't call it incarceration, however; we use the word *resentment,* which literally means "to feel back."

Following his release from the Bastille, Dr. Manette was taken by his daughter Lucie across the channel to England where the beautiful girl gave him her undivided attention. Under this tender care the doctor gradually regained his contact with life and was able to resume his medical practice.

In his bedroom the doctor carefully kept the bench and other shoemaking tools he had used for so many years in the time of his incarceration. When the crisis of Lucie's marriage came, his housekeeper found him sitting in the corner of his room at his bench, working on a shoe—to all intents and purposes back in prison again.

When the doctor recovered from this episode he had no memory of the experience, and his friend, Mr. Lorry, tactfully suggested that it might be advisable to get rid of the shoemaker's bench and tools. Dr. Manette saw the wisdom of this and agreed, providing the removal took place in his absence. So followed the remarkable scene when Mr. Lorry and Miss Pross, the housekeeper, destroyed the bench and buried the tools in the backyard. Never again would Dr. Manette be able to return to the activities of his years of imprisonment.

Many of us are prisoners of the past when we should be living in the present. It is time for us to take the tools of our servitude and destroy them.

How to Take Control of Your Life

1. A Russian once accused a Britisher of mortgaging the present to the past. The Britisher in turn charged the Rus-

sian with sacrificing the present to the future. Let us use the present. Just for today.

2. Take an occasional look back, enjoy the nostalgic moment, then recall all the debits and the unrealities of that moment. Have a fickle love affair with the past.

3. Remember that constantly looking in the rearview mirror will not only give you a crick in the neck, but put you on a collision course in the present.

4. It would be easy to get the idea from our emphasis that man only consists in his behavior. A better statement would be: We are not just our behavior—we are the person managing our behavior.

5. Psychologist Coleman spoke about the third determinant in personality. In addition to an individual's genetic endowment and his physical and sociocultural environment there is the *decision-making self.*

6. When John Glenn went aloft as the first American in orbital flight the vehicle was so automated that it seemed as if Glenn was just going along for the ride. But when the spaceship malfunctioned Glenn took control. No matter what programming has gone on in our lives, we must *take control.*

7. Don't let the "paralysis of analysis" keep you in bondage to the past.

8. Climb every mountain, but make sure you are headed in the right direction.

9. Why not hold a burial service to destroy the bitter resentments that are holding you captive. If we don't destroy and bury them they will destroy and bury us.

Setting Your Family Free

The Resentment Syndrome may be the most important single factor in problem families today, particularly with regard to difficulties in the basic relationship of husbands and wives.

- The resentful person is a reactor rather than an initiator. What other people do determines their attitude in a given situation.
- The word *resent* comes from two Latin words and means, as we have said, "feel back." Resentful people are continually looking back, living in the past.
- A resentful person is imprisoned—captured by an emotion.

The answer to this situation is *action*. Here are four things you should undertake:

1. Remember to forget. The philosopher Kant trusted his servant Lampe for many years. Then he discovered that Lampe had systematically cheated him. He discharged Lampe, but sorely missed him. In his journal he wrote, "Remember to forget Lampe." When you are tempted to dwell on that past event, "remember to forget."

2. Take a positive action. If the memory continues to plague you, focus on your part, small though it may be, that you played. If you took some wrong action at the time or since, undertake a plan of restitution and put it right. An offended conscience can help to keep the past alive.

3. Be an initiator. Don't wallow in your misery. When the memory of the event comes to mind, make a countermove. Use the thought-stopping technique; focus on "stop," say it out loud, shout if you can. Move physically, turn your mind to the good things in your life.

4. Remember the words of a great man: "Nothing on earth consumes a man like resentment."

WE PRIZE OUR FREEDOM ABOVE OUR RESENTMENTS

9
Block Self-Retreat

It is characteristic of anything that moves—any object, person, organization, or game—that in that moving process it gains momentum. William James, the pioneer psychologist, offered a simple explanation for a large portion of that momentum by seeing it as taking place within the individual who then influenced the society around him. He said, "Habits are the flywheel of society." Habits, once established, provide the subject with a source of free energy which maintains his momentum.

Momentum even applies to the basic physiological processes of our bodies. Dennis Weaver, radio and television actor, for many years played the part of the simple-minded stiff-legged Chester in the hayburner "Gunsmoke." Being an amateur psychologist of sorts, Weaver today gives talks, one of which is on the topic, "Habits, Your Master or Your Slave." In that presentation he uses an illustration from his show biz career. "I was on 'Gunsmoke' playing a man with a stiff leg for nine years," he says. "People ask me how I did that; it was just habit—muscle memory."

As Weaver suggests, the momentum that habits give to us can lead us in two directions—upward and downward. The dilemma we face is how to use these forces within our bodies for our advancement, in the development of good, productive habits, and to avoid the enslavement which can come from bad and unprofitable habits.

Two Strategies

Few stories in the annals of the Americas make more interesting reading than the account of the Spanish conquest of Mexico and Peru. These are the records of activity and adventure, and of overcoming adversity. The saga of each is associated with a great leader, Cortez in Mexico, and Pizarro in Peru. They illustrate the capacity to prevent followers from losing momentum by turning to a safer but less desirable way of life, motivating them to make new commitments and move forward.

Planning to Forestall Retreat

Cortez had landed on the American coastline and planned to move into the hinterland to conquer Mexico. Following the landing, his men's enthusiasm for the expedition began to evaporate. He realized the seriousness of the situation when he discovered a group of his followers were planning to seize one of the ships and sail back to Cuba. The leader decided on drastic action. Two ringleaders were sentenced to death, several to whipping, and the pilot who would have charted the course of the ship had his feet cut off. Signing the sentences and death warrants, Cortez was heard to lament, "Would that I had never learned to write."

DECISIVE MOTIVATIONAL ACTION #9

Utilize strategies to fend off any possibility of retreat in your enterprise by ordering your situation so that habit-power will not be misused in bad habits. Learn the techniques necessary to become a habit-creator. As a part of your action program, learn of the benefits of retroflexive reformation.

Yet the presence of the ships provided an ever-present temptation for turning back from the expedition. Cortez arranged for a convenient report stating that the vessels were worm-eaten and no longer seaworthy. On the basis on this contrived document he ordered that the ships should be burned. As the smoke ascended into the sky, his shocked followers loudly protested that their general had led them like cattle to be slaughtered in the shambles. Cortez responded with one of his celebrated speeches in which he pointed out there was no way back to Cuba and they might as well make the most of the situation. In short order his followers were cheering and crying out. "To Mexico! To Mexico!"

What associated thought comes to mind when you hear the word habit? It is probably bad. "Bad habit" is the phrase that comes to most of us. The immediate question is, "How can I handle this mechanism in my personality that can exercise such a control over me?"

Evasive Psychic Self-Mutilation

The answer to the bad-habit problem may be seen in Cortez's punishment of the ship's pilot. As Cortez apparently saw it, this man was going to lead the others on their voyage of retreat, so he was deprived of his feet. It would now be difficult to move anywhere! Jesus, aware of the use of punishments like this in His own day, used the figure of speech, "If thy foot offend thee, cut it off." Of course, this gentlest of all men did not mean it literally. Jesus was speaking about what I like to call Evasive Psychic Self-Mutilation. If you walk someplace where you are likely to be tempted to violate your values, then cut off your foot, don't go there, avoid that situation. When you are tempted to move in the wrong direction, one of the best plans is to order events so that it will not be easy to follow that course of action.

Jesus added two more extensions of the idea and told His followers that if their eye offended they were to pluck it out, and if their hand offended they were to cut it off. Here was the warning against looking at the wrong thing and using the hand for activities that might lead the doer into trouble.

The Internal Tyranny

Habits can exercise a tyrannical control over us. In the turbulent sixties, the cry was "Do it!" "Try it!"—with some tragic results. Some things, like certain drugs, should never be tried because they can all too easily initiate a habit pattern that will enslave the practitioner.

A recent writer on preventive medicine says three things accelerate the aging process: cigarette smoking, inactivity, and obesity. He adds that if you want to extend your life span "... you must eliminate all three of these factors." One

of them, smoking, is a frightening illustration of a habi
holds many people in its iron grip. Sad indeed is the s
tion of a person suffering with emphysema, yet conti
to use the tobacco that caused the condition, pathetical
menting, "I just can't break the habit."

An even more pathetic posture can be seen in the inc
ual who justifies his bondage by asserting he must hav
freedom to do whatever he wants to do.

When Madam Rowland had served her purpose i
French Revolution she was condemned by her erst
comrades to die at the guillotine. As she approache
dread instrument, she paused to kneel at the plaster i
of the god Liberty. Looking up into that unresponsive
she cried out, "Oh liberty, what crimes are committed i
name."

The Apostle Paul stated the situation very clearly, "
do anything I want to if Christ has not said no, but so
these things aren't good for me. Even if I am allowed
them, I'll refuse to if I think they might get such a grip o
that I can't easily stop when I want to" (1 Corinthians
TLB).

Going into Action

What is the answer to the smoking problem? Our pr
tive medicine authority answers, "Stop all at once. Don'
taper off." He confirms the strategy of Jesus, of using
sive Psychic Self-Mutilation, "If thy hand or foot offend
cut them off."

The problem drinker smashes his bottles and learns
productive ways of spending his evenings. The obese pe
fastens a sign on the refrigerator door that reads, "R
your eating habits." The smoker throws away his tob

129

The gambler resigns his club membership. All of these are examples of Evasive Psychic Self-Mutilation.

To ensure that we avoid the tyranny of bad habits, the very best strategy is to engage in some Evasive Psychic Self-Mutilation and stop their momentum.

The Good Habit

We have already noted the unfortunate connotations of the word *habit,* and the way the adjective *bad* is so closely associated with it. This negative connotation may lead us to overlook positive aspects of the habit phenomenon. A closer examination may cause us to reconsider and ultimately conclude that habits, rather than dogs, deserve the title of man's best friend.

Habit-power is strong, but in the best sense of the word it is neutral. It all depends on what use we make of this powerful force. When we realize that habits can be our friends and allies we begin to see how important it is that we take the time to initiate and reinforce good habits.

In the same way that Cortez demonstrated the way to handle the bad-habit attitude, Pizarro teaches us the lesson of initiating a good-habit program. Pizarro, seeking to conquer Peru on the western coast of South America, followed a different course of action than did Cortez on the eastern coast of Mexico. He, too, was faced with the problem of followers who had lost their momentum.

Bogged down with his little band of men on the inhospitable island of Gallo, Pizarro awaited the arrival of ships from Panama which would bring them provisions and take them to the mainland. When two ships did arrive, they brought an order from the governor of Panama directing them to return to that colony. Pizarro decided the time had come for action.

130

A Man More Accustomed to Act than to Talk

The cavalier gathered his little band of ragged followers on the sandy beach and with his sword traced a line on the sand from east to west. Turning to the south he said, "Friends and comrades! On that side are toil, hunger, nakedness, the drenching storm, desertion, and death. On this side ease and pleasure. There lies Peru with its riches; here Panama and its poverty. Choose, each man, what best becomes a brave Castilian. For my part, I go south."

With this statement Pizarro stepped across the line. The pilot Ruiz followed, then twelve other men.

Prescott, the historian, notes that this was the crisis of Pizarro's fate and his action decided his future destiny. The action was characteristic of a man "more accustomed to act rather than to talk."

If we are going to use the wonderful momentum that is resident in our personalities it will require that we become deadly in earnest about this matter of building our habit-power. We must make a commitment, step across the line and launch ourselves on a new adventure.

A Habit Action Program

Why not establish your own habit action program? Remember that we are not only creatures of habit; we are the creators of habits. Our plan will involve a series of steps:

1. Decide on your habit objective.

Let it be a worthy aim that you have in mind, remembering the awesome possibilities. The Duke of Wellington not only defeated Napoleon at the Battle of Waterloo, but was also one of the great personalities of the Victorian era. His insistence on excellence in the British army led to the use of a phrase among the troops for many years after his death. If some work had been done and any doubt remained about its quality, they would say, "It wouldn't have done for the Duke." When the Duke reviewed the use of drill and repetition in army practices he said, "Habit second nature? Habit is ten times nature."

WE ARE NOT ONLY CREATURES OF HABIT
WE ARE ALSO THE CREATORS OF HABITS

I once knew a man of limited ability who developed the capacity to memorize locomotive numbers. He contrasted vividly with a minister of my acquaintance who makes a practice of memorizing the name of every person whom he meets; this skill has greatly extended the scope of his ministry. Decide on a worthy objective.

2. Launch into your enterprise with abandon.

Remember William James's metaphor: Habits are the flywheel of society. A flywheel is an important part of many machines. Once the machine is moving the flywheel keeps it running smoothly and provides the momentum to keep it going.

As a boy I had the responsibility for starting up a one-cylinder internal combustion engine by winding a leather strap around the flywheel. I would tug on that strap while the green monster huffed and puffed, coughed and spluttered. Then it suddenly sprang to life and the humming flywheel gave off a sound that was music to my ears. The flywheel was ready to spin, but it sure took an effort to get it going.

William James maintained that initiating a habit takes energy and enthusiasm. Getting a good start is fundamental. James was almost evangelistic as he urged anyone who wanted to acquire a new habit to let everybody know, to make a public pledge if possible, and order life in such a way that all circumstances would push toward the performance of the habit.

Get truly launched into the new line of activity.

3. Don't allow an exception until the habit is established.

When James pointed out the way in which certain activities are painstakingly learned and then automatically carried on, he said the important goal is, "To make our nervous system our ally instead of our enemy." The smallest unit of the nervous system is the neuron. These neurons are linked together by synaptic connections, tiny gaps over which the neural current must jump as it moves the message to the appropriate muscle. The more frequently the neural current jumps the gap the easier it is on subsequent journeys. Thus is built a neuron memory which is engraved on our nervous system and enables us to automatically carry on the desired activity.

There is a sense in which our nervous system is like a computer. The computer has tremendous power, but it must be programmed. The same is true of our neural system, and the sure way of programming is by constant repetition, not allowing a single exception.

4. Keep your habit in good shape with daily exercise.

Two of the most demanding things a human can do are read

proficiently and knit wool into a garment. I once knew a woman who could do both of these at the same time.

She and I were commuters. We traveled on the same train each day. We never talked because she was busy. She dexterously manipulated four knitting needles at a remarkably fast clip. This in itself would have been a considerable achievement, but in addition she had a book opened on an attaché case on her knees; periodically, she flipped the page as she read.

It was a remarkable performance of two skills, each of which had been acquired at the expense of considerable energy, but were now being carried on effortlessly. The sight of that knitting and the way the lady automatically tugged more wool from its ball reminded me that William James said that when we do not regularly practice a skill it is like dropping a ball of wool which rapidly comes unraveled.

Although we traveled on the same train for some months I never had the opportunity to discuss her skills with this lady. She was too busy keeping them alive and in good shape by daily exercise.

If we realized the extent to which we are mere bundles of habits, we would give more attention to their formation.
William James

Habits That Help Families

Some spiritual habits can be of great value to our family members and they are demonstrated in the habits of Jesus. The Bible tells us that He *learned obedience.* He acquired three habits that would be of great value to our family members today.

1. Attending worship. He went "as usual into the synagogue . . ." (Luke 4:16 TLB). The indication of the verse is that this was His regular practice. So today, a family that attends worship as a group builds a sense of togetherness. One trait of a healthy family as shown by a recent survey is "a shared religious core."

2. Praying. "He [Jesus] left the upstairs room and went as usual to the Mount of Olives. . . . and prayed . . ." (Luke 22:39,41 TLB). Note the "as usual"—it was part of His regular practice. The rather trite saying that the family that prays together stays together is much more than that and points toward a significant possibility for families that want to rise to new levels. Unless we have that within us which is above us, we become like that which is about us.

3. Reading the Scriptures. When Jesus went to the synagogue it was for a specific purpose: ". . . [He] stood up to read" (Luke 4:16 TLB). Jesus showed a remarkable knowledge of the Old Testament and quoted it with consummate ease. Apparently He had developed the habit of reading it and spent many hours with the Book. The same habit will have its rewards for us.

Train up a child in the way he should go—and walk there yourself once in a while.

Josh Billings

Keep Your Experience by Giving It Away

In the course of the Spanish campaign to conquer Mexico a message had come to headquarters from two groups of people. They were each living about thirty miles away, in different directions, and each indicated they were in grave danger from the incursion of hostile neighbors. They desperately needed assistance. The fortunes of the Spaniards at this time were at a low ebb. They were, in the words of one historian, "In a condition to receive rather than to give help."

The officers discussed the requests and reached a consensus. Because of the weakened condition of their forces it would be unwise, they concluded, to further deplete their strength by sending the requested assistance. However, the commanding general overruled their counsel by presenting another perspective: "The greater our weakness, the greater need we have to cover it under a show of strength."

Two good-sized bodies of soldiers were dispatched with orders to complete their task and be back in camp within ten days. This they did. A few days later, ambassadors from the defeated territories arrived seeking an alliance with the victors and bringing troops to join with the Spaniards.

The Helper-Therapist Principle

The action of the Spanish forces in moving out to assist when they were somewhat uncertain of their own condition may be an example of what some psychologists call the "helper-therapist principle." In its simplest form this principle may be stated: It frequently happens that *those who help others are often helped most themselves.* It has been asserted that, "In a group in which Criminal A joins with some noncriminals to change Criminal B, it is probably more effective in changing Criminal A than Criminal B."

This use of the principle is sometimes called "retroflexive reformation." Using this technique, the strategy is to make the person who is helping, and thus the agent of change, into the target of change. Alcoholics Anonymous, one of the most successful of the self-help groups, makes much of this giving principle. One of their pungent sayings is, "You cannot keep your experience unless you give it away."

Six values come to a person who does not necessarily have every aspect of his own problem under control, but is willing to help someone else who is having a similar struggle. These include a sense of independence, an involvement in a laboratory experience, a subjective reaction of well-being, a subtle exercise of self-persuasion, an experience of social interchange, and an involvement in learning through teaching. These will each repay our attention.

A Sense of Independence

The helper who undertakes to assist another individual becomes a more independent person himself. He may have been used to receiving help from a counselor. He has experienced the almost inevitable tendency to look upon the counselor as an authority figure. This sometimes has the effect of making the counselee dependent and unsure about spreading his own wings and accepting responsibility for his own actions.

Now, as a helper, he has to make decisions as to what should be done next. He makes these decisions and has a sense of being capable of independent action.

In any type of counseling it is important that the counselee should become independent. The sweetest words to a counselor's ear are, "I think I can now manage by myself." Working as a helper develops this very desirable sense of independence.

Involvement in a Laboratory Setting

While helping another person, the helper is involved in a laboratory experience in which he can frequently see his own problem being acted out by someone else. Within himself he is able to see his own problem at a distance and often identifies with the situation of this other person. Carried out by someone else, he is able to see that this behavior is so obviously nonproductive.

As a therapist I have often had occasion to realize this. My wife tells me, "When you are deeply involved in helping people having difficulty with their marriages, you are a much better husband and father." This is a common experience of people who work in a helping role as they participate in the laboratory of experience. Helping others, the helper is also a helpee.

A Sense of Well-Being

As a result of helping someone else the helper is often the recipient of a sense of well-being. As one man put it, "It feels good to be a helper; it increases my sense of control, of being valued, of being capable."

Mrs. Harrison is the wife of a retired college professor. In her church she works in the college department and she and her husband spend a lot of time entertaining students in their home. The result is that they never seem to have any privacy; students are coming and going and eating. Living on a fixed retirement income, they admit that this activity sometimes puts strains on their budget.

During a conversation with them about their entertaining activities, I had a growing sense that the students were taking advantage of these two generous people. I asked the lady how she felt about the situation. To my amazement the good woman with shining eyes responded, "It is such a privilege to be able to do this."

I MUST BE BETTER WHEN I CAN HELP SOMEONE ELSE

One man who was working on his own problem and who had moved into the role of helper in a therapy group stated his perception of the experience this way: "I must be much better when I am able to help someone else." Involvement in the function of helping and a sense of accomplishment builds up self-confidence and ego strength.

A Subtle Experience of Self-Persuasion

Self-persuasion becomes a factor. A research project compares the results to be gained from two different activities—reading material on a subject as compared with delivering a speech advocating a certain position. The findings indicated that the students who delivered the speech showed a much greater commitment to that particular point of view than those who merely read the material.

Knute Rockne, the fabled Notre Dame football coach, was not only a remarkable motivator of his team. He also accomplished some unwitting objectives. On one occasion his team was losing the ball game and, with halftime in the offing, he searched his mind for some dynamic message to take to his players in the locker room.

He shared his concern with a friend who stood at his side. The friend responded that it might be a good idea to tell the team that the eastern alumni were against him and that if the team lost the match he might lose his job as coach.

The suggestion appealed to Rockne. He prepared himself and at the half went into the locker room and delivered one of his famous exhortations. His presentation was convincing and his players, out of concern for their coach, went out with a completely new spirit and won the game.

Traveling back on the train that evening, Rockne and his friend discussed the game, play-by-play, and gave particular attention to way the team had played in the second half. Rockne suddenly said, "What's more, I'm going to write those eastern alumni and demand an apology from them." Rockne had effectively convinced himself in his efforts to motivate his football team. He became an example of self-persuasion through persuading others.

An Experience of Social Exchange

Social exchange is involved when one person helps another. When one individual assists another, there is generally no exchange of money. Instead, there is a social exchange.

This social exchange has a remarkable outcome as helper and helpee give to each other without either person losing anything. Not only are there no losers, but both helper and helpee are gainers in the situation. Some call this the Double Win.

Learning through Teaching

The teacher learns as he endeavors to teach others. A number of studies have been carried out that show that in the process of teaching others, the teacher may learn as much as the student.

Of course it is not a twentieth-century discovery that children can teach each other, for history tells us that as far into the past as ancient Rome, children were taught by their peers. The modern discovery is that in the process the children who are tutoring are probably learning more than their pupils.

In the process of teaching another person there are certain cognitive gains. The material has to be learned, reviewed, prepared, reformulated, organized, and examples and illustrations provided.

During World War II, at the time of the introduction of radar, a young recruit struggled to grasp the principles of electronics. When he finally managed to graduate from electronics school, his command assigned him to a teaching position. Toiling to simplify the concepts while teaching, he wrote a book on the subject. The writing was so successful that he ultimately became a full-time author and an authority in the field. Teaching others, he made some important discoveries for himself.

The Christian Perspective

For Christians, the concept of giving away to gain is easily understandable. Jesus stated it very clearly: "Whosoever will save his life shall lose it; but whosoever shall lose his life for my sake and the gospel's, the same shall save it" (Mark 8:35). In Paul's address to the Ephesian elders he reminded them of an unwritten saying of Jesus, "It is more blessed to give than to receive" (Acts 20:35).

At a meeting of a group working on weight reduction, Jean is telling her story. Despite her efforts at reducing Jean is still pretty solid and has obviously not found it easy to diet. With a smile on her face she tells her story: "I got to feeling hungry and decided I was weak and needed something to eat. So I got out the peanut butter and made myself the biggest sandwich. It looked so good.

"The phone rang and I heard the voice of my buddy Joan.

"Joan was having a hard time. Just as she was about to make herself a sundae, she thought of me and decided to seek my help.

"I really went to work on Joan. I told her how well she had been doing and how dangerous it would be for her to eat that sundae.

"As I hung up the phone, I reached over and pushed my peanut butter sandwich into the garbage pail."

Jean had saved herself by helping her buddy.

Christians across the years have faced the challenge that their attitudes toward their material possessions are an indicator of their attitude of faith. They have discovered the truth of the John Bunyan verse:

> There was a man,
> Folks thought him mad,
> The more he gave,
> The more he had.

Modeling for the Family

One of the best ways for a family member to help other family members is by giving his experience away in a technique known as modeling.

The word *teach* means to show, and the best teaching is frequently done by demonstration. So has come the concept of teaching sometimes referred to as "imitative learning," "observational learning," or "modeling."

Traditionally we have stated that people learn by trial and error; but we know that many skills, such as performing surgery, cannot be learned this way. In an instance like this the student must watch someone else perform the skill before attempting it.

The method is not really new. Jesus Christ was the great Example. Faced with some bickering among His disciples He took a basin and towel and washed their feet. When He had finished, He said, "If I, then, your Lord and Master, have washed your feet, ye also ought to wash one another's feet. For I have given you an example, that ye should do as I have done to you" (John 13:14,15).

This same note is to be found in many other parts of the New Testament. Barclay calls it the ethic of imitation. This imitation ethic is of special importance in family life.

Lowell Thomas told the story of the attempts of the British to build a road through the fabled Khyber Pass. The laborers found themselves under constant harassment from a sharp-shooter in the mountains. A company of British soldiers were brought in, but they were unsuccessful in tracking down the sharpshooter.

Deciding to try new tactics, they offered a reward to any Indian laborer who could bring the sharpshooter back dead or alive. A slip of a boy volunteered and was given rifle and ammunition. He disappeared into the mountains. A single shot was heard, and the next day he came down the mountainside pulling the dead body of a man.

The soldiers gathered around the boy and eagerly demanded, "How did you get him?"

The boy looked at the body for a moment and then responded, "I knew all his little tricks. He's my father."

All the family members are teachers and sometimes the most potent lessons are taught when we are least aware.

His little arms crept round my neck,
And then I heard him say,
Four simple words I shan't forget,
Four words that made me pray,

143

They turned a mirror on my soul,
On secrets no one knew,
They startled me, I hear them yet,
He said,
"I'll be like you."

HE WHO UNDERTAKES TO TEACH ANOTHER PERSON DISCOVERS HE LEARNS MORE THAN HE TEACHES

10
You Are What You Do

As go our actions, so go our feelings or emotions.

Diebert and Harmon

Mr. Lorry is preparing Miss Manette for the moment of reunion with her father whom she has never seen. Representing Telford's Bank, he is trying to impress on her that he is an impartial businessman and says, "Feelings, I have no time for them. I have no feelings, I am a mere machine."

Poor Mr. Lorry, the man without feelings. He makes a vivid contrast with Father Damien, who stepped in to fill the missionary vacancy left by the death of his brother. On the island of Molokai, he served the leper colony as both physician and priest. Then came the never-to-be-forgotten day when, while working in the kitchen, he accidentally spilled boiling water over his hand—and felt nothing. Now he knew. He was leprous. The loss of feeling indicated the impending loss of life.

145

"Happy are they that mourn (feel)"—Jesus

Few of us would ever want to live a dull, grey, monotonous life without feelings—no highs or lows, ups or downs, sunlight and shadows.

DECISIVE MOTIVATIONAL ACTION #10

Challenge the notion, *man is what he feels,* with the action concept, *man is what he does.* Master the action-feeling sequence—perceive . . . act . . . feel—and learn how you can get off the emotional roller coaster.

Within the inner sanctum of our personality, emotional reactions provide some of our highest and lowest spots. We greet each other on this level:

"How are you feeling?"

"If I felt any better I couldn't stand it."

"I feel like a million dollars."

"I feel awful."

"I feel as if I could die."

But it is possible to have too much of a good thing. So much have we come to value these experiences that we have become a nation of emotional indulgers. Crying over soap operas. Paying good money to watch horror movies that scare the daylights out of us. Yelling for joy while men battle each other to a bloody pulp in the ring. Popping uppers and downers. Letting it all hang out in so-called "sensitivity" groups that may be the most insolent attack ever launched on people's finer feelings.

In the milder manifestations these feelings include elation, excitement, anxiety, fear, apprehension. The more serious gyrations of the emotional life range all the way from the dark depths of depression to the excited elation of mania or the oscillating, shattering manic depressive psychosis.

What Is Man?

Man is what he thinks. "I think, therefore I am."—Descartes.

"Man is what he eats."—Feuerbach.

Man is what he feels. "I feel, therefore I am."—Satyr.

Man is what he does. "I act, therefore I am."—Mowrer.

Man is what he says. "What the tongue is, the man is."—Madame Defarge.

Of these options the most widely accepted, but not necessarily correct, would probably be
MAN IS WHAT HE FEELS.

Should You Express Your Emotions?

When it comes to dealing with emotions, even the exponents of the newer behavioral techniques are on the horns of a dilemma. A good proportion of these are under the sway of the catharsis idea, the notion that expressing emotions is not only good but in some instances absolutely essential.

One author states, "The expression of anger is a healthy thing," and claims that people who learn his technique can help others "... express anger in nondestructive ways." The implication of these techniques is that anger must be expressed and if it isn't ventilated there is a danger of a destructive manifestation in such forms as migraine headaches, asthma, ulcers, skin problems.

Practice Makes Perfect

The alleged value of the expression of anger is a very doubtful proposition and overlooks the possibility that expression of anger may be a learned self-perpetuating behavior.

A child given to fits of rage early learns to "control by tantrum." As these expressions bring responses of awe and submission from others, he is reinforced in his primitive outbursts and continues to use them as a means of control. Somewhere along the line he must discover that civilized people prefer verbal problem solving as a way of handling life's difficulties and his outbursts are futile and, in fact, self-defeating.

There are reasons for doubting the catharsis argument that emotions are "drained off" by expression. A salesman attending a conference being addressed by a psychologist was given to fiery outbursts during the discussion periods. He later sought a private interview with the psychologist who in the course of their discussion gently chided him for his vehement statements. The salesman responded, "But you psychologists are always telling us not to 'bottle up' anger and so I just go ahead and express my emotions."

The psychologist asked a simple question: "Does expressing your emotions mean you are more in control of your anger?"

Looking somewhat crestfallen the salesman responded, "No. I'm afraid I'm getting worse. My boiling point seems to be getting lower all the time."

In terms of the decisive motivational action he was practicing the wrong skill. If practice really makes perfect he was fast becoming adept at angry responses.

What Anger Accomplishes

There are at least three bad results from expression of anger. As we have already noted, the subject learns and practices an antisocial skill as he indulges in his outbursts of anger.

In the second place he alienates the objects of his wrath and the observers of the experience and so comes to live an increasingly isolated existence as people learn to avoid him.

Thirdly—one of the most ironic aspects of the attitude of a person hostile toward another individual—he damages himself internally. John Hunter, the great anatomist, said, "My life is in the hands of any villain who cares to annoy me." Anger can take its toll of the human frame.

The idea that "man is what he feels" has ushered in a new reign of psychological terror. Resentful people, for example, may be completely immobilized by emotional reactions to some event in the distant past which is keeping them in subjection at this moment.

AS GO OUR ACTIONS SO GO OUR FEELINGS
OR EMOTIONS

In an era in which emotions reign supreme, emotional reactions become the new dictatorial dominating forces to
which the subject must submit. The actionist completely rejects this notion and comes forth with the concept of another way.

"I want to apologize. . . ." The young man is standing before a group of residents in the "house," a self-help community of drug addicts. The young man has been in trouble and
his fellow house members have confronted him and admin-
istered discipline by demoting him to one of the low status
positions within the community.

He says, "I want to apologize to the house. I want to apologize for indulging—and I commit myself to stop it."

What was this man indulging himself in—drugs, alcohol,
stealing money?

No, none of these. He has been gloomy, glum, and depressed. Instead of saying he has been in the grip of some ir-
resistible impersonal force, he says he has been "indulging."
He is accepting a measure of responsibility for his depression.

William James used a practical illustration to make a
point. He said a man was walking through the woods and,
meeting a bear, he began to run. What was the sequence?
Did he become frightened and turn and run, or did he turn
and run and then become frightened? James indicated the
possibility of what I am calling the Action Principle, that we
can be responsible for our emotions which may follow
rather than precede action.

The pioneer psychologist stated, "There is, accordingly,
no better known or more generally useful precept in the

moral teaching of youth, or in one's personal self-discipline, than that which bids us pay primary attention to what we do and express, and not care too much for what we feel. . . . Action seems to follow feelings, but really action and feeling go together; and by regulating the action, which is under the more direct control of the will, we can indirectly regulate the feeling, which is not."

REGULATING THE ACTION, WE CAN INDIRECTLY REGULATE THE EMOTIONS

The paradigm of two contrasting approaches to emotion would be:

NOT   Perceive→Feel→Act

BUT   Perceive→Act →Feel

Partial confirmation of this approach comes from the peer-group psychotherapy approach, especially in working with drug abusers who are specialists in seeking emotional highs. One group says, "We can't stop feeling, but we can direct behavior."

It is much easier to act yourself into a new way of feeling than to feel yourself into a new way of acting.
E. Stanley Jones

A second statement of a self-help group is, "Do the thing and the rewards will emerge." Although an individual's emotional reactions are complex and the drug abuser is willing to put his very life at risk to get the chemical assistance that will give him his high, there is a fairly simple way in which the whole matter can be brought under control. This method is action—*an action that will bring peace of mind.*

Look who's teaching the Bible!

In the burgeoning interest in Bible study, a wide variety of groups in offices, schools, and homes have sprung up with people seeking to practice the teachings of this fascinating book. Preeminent among these is Alcoholics Anonymous who, while not engaging in formal Bible study, are nevertheless emphasizing the frequently overlooked biblical teaching of restitution.

The all-important principle of restitution is declared in two of their "Twelve Steps":

- Made a list of the people we had harmed and became willing to make amends to them.
- Made direct amends to such people wherever possible.

This nonchurch group is recalling us to the biblical idea of restitution, or putting back, which is a decisive motivational action. It is not easy to go to another person and confess that you have wronged him and that you have now come to put things right. But the action must be taken. A guilty conscience can have a devastating effect on the emotional life of the individual. Depression is a characteristic manifestation of guilt.

We know that God alone can forgive sin and the means of this forgiveness is faith in Christ. Yet even after such a wonderful experience as this, some people will say, "I do not *feel* forgiven." A wide counseling experience has taught me that these people frequently need to do something—to undertake an act of restitution. Following this, they feel better. The act of restitution gives the individual peace of mind.

The Creative Expression of Emotion

There is a creative expression of emotion. It is in action. Psychologists have long spoken about sublimation, the redirection of primitive energies into a creative channel. The best single way to drain off emotions is to exercise.

News has come of a Japanese factory which placed in the plant a life-sized rubber figure fashioned like the supervisor. A frustrated worker can take out his hostile feelings on that representation of his frustrations. But what of the supervisor himself? One of the best pieces of counsel to the harassed supervisor would be that instead of going straight home and possibly displacing his anger on his wife and children, he should go to the gymnasium or the swimming pool, or jog or walk home, and so release his built-up annoyances.

Those Powerful Endorphins

Not only does exercise release built-up emotions; it also allows the body to release its own powerful mood elevators. It has long been known that people who engage in hard exercise are often elated by the experience. Now has come an explanation for this.

When the body is exercised vigorously, the pituitary gland releases endorphins which have been likened to morphine. Kenneth Cooper, the exercise specialist, claims endorphins might be as much as two hundred times more powerful than morphine in creating a natural high.

It has long been noted that an injured athlete can continue to play without any apparent pain. One player was found to have a fractured bone the evening following the game. Apparently the endorphin level in his body, raised by his vigorous action, protected him from pain during the game.

153

People suffering with depression may have low endorphin levels and the natural treatment for them would be exercise. Some physicians are saying that exercise is nature's tranquilizer. It is just waiting to be used and it is free.

Do the thing you fear and the death of fear is certain.
—Emerson

One of the scariest things for many people is to stand before an audience and make a speech. What should you do?

A man who in his lifetime listened to and criticized over 150,000 speeches in a forty-year period explained: "You are afraid to talk. You feel you will fail. You failed because you failed before, so you built a habit of failure."

Dale Carnegie's suggestion was to gather a number of friends together and try talking to them. Seek every opportunity to speak. Little by little, confidence will grow by speaking. Carnegie suggested an action program and laid down this principle, "Cure yourself of your fear of speaking by speaking." He was working on Emerson's principle—"do the thing you fear and the death of fear is certain."

The Tyrant Is Vanquished

The good news is that our lives do not have to be lived under the domination of our emotions. We are challenged to step out and take control. The way of control is the way of action.

The vestibule of the residency in Salzburg, Austria is where many of Mozart's works were originally performed. Being present for an anniversary performance in this setting, with attendants in long red coats, bejewelled women, distinguished men wearing the sashes of their order, and a ceremonial lighting of the candles, was like going back to another age. On the ceiling of that ornate room is a beautiful mural depicting Alexander taming the horse Bucephalus. This magnificent animal was considered untamable, but as the youthful Alexander watched the trainers at work he realized that the horse was frightened of its own shadow.

Climbing onto the animal's back he turned its head to the sun, ordered the handlers to release it and drove in the spurs. Unable to see its shadow it ran under his urging until it was ultimately tamed. The horse Bucephalus became a legend, and was so important to Alexander that when it died during a campaign in India, Alexander had the animal buried and changed the name of the city to Bucephalus in the horse's honor.

Alexander had one dark blot on his life. While arguing with his companion Clitus he lost his temper and killed him. Alexander's biographer commented that he who was able to conquer the world militarily could not rule his own spirit. Like the untamed Bucephalus, uncontrolled emotions can dominate and destroy us, but once tamed and disciplined, they can open undreamed possibilities for us.

Psychosomatic or Somatopsychic

The time has come for us to learn a new word. We have long known the term *psychosomatic* which comes from two Greek words meaning body and soul and is used to describe the intimate relationship between the body and the emotions. Psychosomatic is generally used to refer to the way the emotions affect the body. Many people who are sitting in doctors' offices have nothing physically wrong with them. Their illnesses are described as "functional" or "psychogenic" and the implication is that the emotional condition of the individual is causing his body to malfunction.

The word *somatopsychic* presents us with another aspect of the body-emotions relationship and indicates the way in which the body influences the emotions. By controlling our bodies we can control our emotions. No matter how depressed we may feel we can take certain action, and in taking these actions make errant emotions come to heel.

Take a somatopsychic approach to your emotional life and you'll have a wonderful new weapon in the struggle against anxiety and depression.

EMOTIONAL MANAGEMENT CALLS FOR DECISIVE MOTIVATIONAL ACTIONS

1. Refuse to let anger and temper dominate you.

2. Learn to dissipate emotion by engaging in creative activities.

3. Realize your physical health may be damaged by rampant emotions.

4. Don't surrender to emotional domination. Accept responsibility for your own emotional control.

5. Practice the James dictum: "By regulating the action, which is under the more direct control of the will, we can indirectly regulate the feeling, which is not."

6. Come to terms with guilt emotions by making restitution. AA steps will make an excellent starting point:

   a. Made a list of the people we had harmed and became willing to make amends to them.

   b. Made direct amends to such people wherever possible.

7. Discipline your fears by challenging them.

8. Build up nature's tranquilizer. Your endorphin level can be raised with a program of exercise.

Family Mental Health

The family is not only responsible for the physical health and well-being of its members but is also obligated to see that the mental health of the group is maintained. Each individual in the family unit has certain needs and these should be met by the functioning family unit.

The psychologist Maslow says that man is a perpetually wanting individual who has a number of needs. They are physiological needs, safety needs, love needs, esteem needs, and self-actualization needs. Life is like climbing a series of steps. We commence with physiological needs, but once these have been satisfied the next set emerges and so on.

The way in which these needs are met in the family is illustrated in the following chart.

The Satisfaction of Needs in the Family Context

Needs	Example	Family Activities
Physiological needs	*Satisfying hunger thirst sex needs*	*Providing shelter Good nutrition Father and mother to have adequate sex life*
Safety Needs	*Desire to live in an orderly world.*	*No intense arguments Absence of physical violence No threats to leave Giving a sense of security*

Needs	Example	Family Activities
Love needs	Sense of being loved	Father and mother make loving gestures to each other Children are included in physical contact, such as hugging each other Love is frequently verbalized, "I love you"
Esteem needs	Having a sense of importance	Father and mother motivate family members to: • Not downgrade each other • Not make unflattering comparisons • Emphasize each person's strong points, particularly in the presence of others • Try to ignore the weak points
Self-actualization needs	Achieving one's potential	The climate of the family should encourage: • mother to develop interests outside the house or her job

- *father to move
  beyond his
  work to hobbies
  or some other
  interests*
- *Children to
  widen their per-
  spectives by
  summer camps,
  special courses,
  use of com-
  puters, etc.*

Our ultimate aim as a family must always be to help all the family members to achieve their potential in self-actualization and religious experience.

11
Act As If

An adolescent boy was a casual visitor to the theater until an incident in one performance. The play was "Hamlet" and there came a dramatic moment when the actor, portraying the ghost, said, "Revenge his foul and most unnatural murder." Drawing his sword, he scraped it across the floor of the stage, making a strange, weird noise which to the youthful watcher sounded like the hell from which the ghost had come.

The sound overwhelmed the young man. His heart beating wildly, he said within himself: *If only I could be an actor. If only I could have a sword and scratch it on the floor.*

IF ONLY!!

The boy who dreamed his adolescent fantasy translated his vision into action and ultimately became one of the greatest actors of all time; the name Sir Ralph Richardson is synonymous with great Shakespearean acting.

The action premise has an imaginative component to it that is triggered by an "if." Kipling expressed it, "If you can dream and not make dreams your master. . . ." In this chapter we are going to consider the possibility of imagination linked with action. It is stated in the phrase, "Act as if."

DECISIVE MOTIVATIONAL ACTION #11

Discover new and exciting ideas, learn new skills, realize hitherto unrealized potentialities, gain new confidence, build new strengths into your marriage relationship, by using the "act as if" technique.

Dr. Ignaz Philipp Semmelweis approached the maternity hospital where he worked and saw a woman in the throes of labor pains lying on the sidewalk, pleading with well-meaning onlookers not to take her into the hospital. Her reason: so many women died there.

The doctor pondered the situation. There were too many deaths, and almost invariably the women in the first clinic were the victims rather than those treated in the second clinic. Why was the record of the second clinic so good, and the first so bad, he pondered.

The eager young doctor diligently investigated and compared the two clinics. Patients were similar, as were food and medical attention. Then he noted a difference in the students attending the women. Those in the first clinic came straight from the dissecting room where they had been working on cadavers.

Semmelweis decided this was the possible cause. His second decision was to *act as if* the students were carrying the infection on their hands. He established a clinic in which the medical attendants carefully washed their hands before examining the patients, and childbirth fever was brought under control. A physician who *acted as if* had done a great service for mankind in general and childbearing women in particular.

Learning New Skills

How will a woman who is having difficulty coping with a family situation learn to gain a new ability?

By learning to *act as if.*

Mrs. Simpson, a reluctant parent, is attending a special class on child raising. She pours out her resentment: "I never wanted to be a mother. The kids completely frustrate me; I feel as if I'm giving them the best years of my life and then they'll be up and gone." She pauses, looks around, and then says, "I know I'm not supposed to say this, but I hate kids."

The psychologist hears her out, then gently reminds her that many people feel the same way as she. He then reads a statement from a book on behavior modification: "You must take the role of an actor, playing at being a positive parent. . . ."

"Take the role of an actor. . . ." Kathie Simpson has been introduced to the concept of *act as if* and there is a good chance that once she has really tried this she will discover that effective behavior brings its own peculiar satisfactions. Once behavior has been established it has rewards, and as the behavior is practiced it gains a certain momentum of its own.

The Politician Who Became a Saint

Thomas à Becket was no actor, but he became an example of the *act as if* principle. Appointed chancellor of England by King Henry II, he was a master diplomat, a brilliant soldier who led the British forces to victory in France, a lover of the finer things in life with a passion for hunting and hawking. Although nominally a deacon of the church he insisted that the church submit itself to the king's demands.

In the year 1162 the archbishop of Canterbury died and King Henry made a rather obvious political move by having Becket installed as the new archbishop, the nominal head of the Church in England. He also secured a papal dispensation which would have allowed Becket to have continued as chancellor as well.

Becket rejected the offer of the dispensation and turned his back on the luxurious living that had previously characterized his life. He became a devout servant of the church. When conflict arose as to the authority of the king in ecclesiastical matters Becket refused to take the compliant role Henry had expected. Stunned by Becket's refusal to bow to his will the king in a petulant moment cried out, "Will no one rid me from this troublesome priest." Whereupon, four of his courtiers departed for Canterbury where they murdered Becket as he prayed before the high altar of the cathedral.

Thomas à Becket was declared a saint in 1172, and is England's preeminent saint. The subject of many writings, it was to his shrine the pilgrims were going in Chaucer's "Canterbury Tales."

What had happened to Becket? When he was appointed to the powerful position of chancellor of England, he acted like a chancellor, using his position to acquire wealth and exploiting the possibilities of his relationship to the king. He lived a life of self-indulgence that he felt appropriate to being a chancellor.

One dramatization of the life of Becket tells of King Henry's rather cavalier announcement to Becket that he intended to make his chancellor the archbishop. Becket's response was, "Please do not do this to me, my lord." He gave the impression that he feared what might be the outcome of the appointment.

Once appointed to the archbishopric, Becket *acted as if* he were an archbishop. He declined the opportunity to continue as chancellor and become a devout and conscientious clergyman. As the archbishop he developed a new sense of loyalty to the church rather than to the king.

When the crisis came and he had to choose between the king and the church he chose the church and ultimately paid with his life. *Acting as if* demands commitment. It is costly because it demands a whole new way of life, but the rewards are great.

Coping with a Threatening Situation

Lovers of the musical play have long enjoyed the adaptation of the book *Anna and the King of Siam* into "The King and I." The story centers on the experiences of an English schoolteacher who has accepted a position as teacher to the children of the royal household.

As the ship sails up the river to the city of Bangkok, the widow teacher is being warned by the ship's captain about the dangers that she as a woman will face in the court of an oriental monarch. His warning is interrupted by the news that a boat with an enormous dragon's head at the bow, and propelled by half-naked natives, is approaching. The captain

warns her that the man sitting under the canopy is the Kra-
lahome or prime minister, adding rather ominously, "That
man has power, and he can use it for you or against you."

Louis, the teacher's small son, is repelled by the sight and
says, "The prime minister is naked." He moves closer to his
mother and in his prim English manner says, "They all look
rather horrible, don't they, Mother?"

The Best Way to Make a Fool of Yourself

What will this eighteenth century teacher-mother do
about such a threatening situation? She *acts as if.*

Her plan is the essence of simplicity. She whistles, holds
her head erect, strikes a careless pose, and convinces everybody that she is not afraid. The bottom line to *acting as if* is
that you not only fool other people—you fool yourself as
well.

Drug addiction may be society's single most difficult problem. Many efforts have been made to cope with it, but with
very little success. Facing the fact that an addict is often a
sociopathic personality, a self-centered, immature con artist,
one experimental group launched an innovative program by
undertaking the difficult task of developing a value system in
an addict. The basic beginning objective was to teach the addict to "grow up" and accept responsibility for himself and
for his behavior. The counsel given to the inmate was, "You
must *act as if* you understand, *act as if* you are a man, *act as
if* you want to do the right thing, *act as if* you care about
other people, *act as if* you are a mature human being."

A similar program, although not for drug addicts, makes
this same emphasis and reminds the participants that their
present way of life is unsatisfactory. They have a chance of

learning a whole new way of life, they are told. The proposition is that they might not believe it, but they are to accept it intellectually. They are exhorted, "Say to yourself, 'I'm going to *act as if* he knows what he's talking about.'" The first step of this experience is *acting as if*. The program involved group therapy procedures, a process of starting from the bottom and working up through ever-expanding responsibilities and opportunities to work for others. Nevertheless at the heart of it stood the program of action which called for a wide use of the *act as if* principle.

No Stunt Men

Our discussion of acting reminds us that our sedentary society is enamored of the idea of conflict and loves to see real action. The immense popularity of football, sometimes described as twenty-two men on the field, struggling and in need of a rest, watched by 60,000 fans, badly in need of exercise, is evidence of this love of action. So also is the appeal of the wrestling match, in which the participants perpetrate acts of physical violence on one another, while making sure that nobody gets hurt.

Hollywood has realized the appeal of action. Movies and TV shows are portraying ever increasingly greater amounts of it in the stories of police, private detectives, paramilitary forces, spies, hired killers, and terrorists. Scenes include such things as automobiles colliding, leaping into the air, crashing down embankments, running down hapless pedestrians—men fighting, wrestling, jumping from hovering helicopters, and rolling cars to fiery explosions.

The craze for ever more spectacular stunts has led to increasingly dangerous actions such as that in which an actor and two children were killed when a hovering helicopter fell on them. A twenty-six-year-old actress doubling for the star was crippled for life after her car in a special scene went zigzagging through the traffic to a head-on collision. One authority has commented that the pressure is on to provide viewers with ever bigger vicarious thrills.

This desire for action without participation has led to the burgeoning role of the stunt man in movies and TV. To meet this demand, the Motion Picture and Television Stunt Academy was formed to train people for this spectacular but dangerous occupation. Students in this institution go through a program that has been described as a cross between marine recruit training and a crash course in antisocial behavior.

When the movie is being filmed, the stunt man steps in and doubles for the actor in the violent action scene. As the filming progresses, the moment of action comes and the call "cut," when the actor moves out and the stunt man steps in. Then comes the call, "action." Once the difficult or dangerous segment is filmed the call is "cut" and the actor takes up his part again—which is about the way many people want to live their lives. They want action—providing that someone else can do it for them.

We reject this premise for the living of life. You cannot do it vicariously—you must act. Not, "I cannot do this. Let me watch someone else do it." But, "I don't think I can do this but I am going to *act as if* I can and throw myself into this role. No stunt men for me."

Playing a Part in Marriage

The *act as if* formula has awesome possibilities for helping troubled marriages. When David McGinnis talked with his counselor he said, "The difficulty is, there's nothing left in my marriage. The magic is gone. We don't have a marriage. I don't love my wife. I used to, but it's all gone now. There's nothing left."

After considerable discussion, the counselor tried to conclude the session by suggesting some activity. He came up with an idea: "Why not try to do something. *Act as if* you did love your wife. Give her the same attention as you did when you were courting her."

There's a good chance that if David followed this counsel and really *acted as if* he were courting his wife a strange change would take place.

Some will object to this counsel on the basis of honesty. David might have said, "I couldn't do that. Don't you guys believe in honesty? I'd be giving a false impression to my wife. It would be deceptive."

David has raised a very interesting point. If he is trying to manipulate his wife so that he can persuade her to do something that he wants, it is deceptive. If, on the other hand, he *acts as if* because he sincerely wants to learn a new way to accept his responsibilities, he is manipulating himself and as a teaching process that is good.

Act as if to deceive—wrong!

Act as if to learn—good.

Being Scientific

Sam Shoemaker put it another way. Asked on one occasion if *acting as if* were not a hypocritical attitude, he answered that a scientist believes a hypothesis is true for long enough to prove whether it is actually so or not. To take an *act as if* stance is to enter an experiment with an open and honest mind. Shoemaker further added that there is a point when an *experiment* can easily become an *experience*.

Probably the greatest religious essayist of all time, Dr.

F. W. Boreham, learned at least one of his superb communication skills by *acting as if*. As a young man he had taken the long trip from England to New Zealand to become the pastor of the Mosgiel Church. He was befriended by a seasoned veteran of the ministry named J. J. Doke, who later became such an influence in the life of Mahatma Gandhi. J. J. Doke was visiting the Boreham home one day when a messenger arrived to summon the young pastor to the home of Nell Gillespie, a parishioner, who was dying.

The youthful minister turned to the veteran and told how troubled he was about his difficult task. Doke suggested that Boreham might *act as if*.

"*Act as if* by imagining that I am Nellie Gillespie and I have sent for you. Speak to me as you would speak to her."

Boreham went out and returned to the room, greeting and talking to Doke the way he intended to approach and speak with the dying girl.

"Too theological, too long," said Doke. "Try again."

Boreham made a second attempt.

"Still too long. Remember, I am weak. Make it simpler still."

The young minister went through it all a third time.

"Excellent. You are ready. God bless you in your important ministry."

Dr. Boreham, one of the greatest communicators in the history of the Christian church, learned one of his basic skills by *acting as if*.

The Most Important Experience of All

The *act as if* principle has a significant application to the spiritual experiences of life. One young man confessed, "For years I tried to find God by reason and logic. I could find no reason for believing. Then someone told me to *act as if* God existed and see what would happen.

"I did, and prayer has become a real, life-giving force to me. I live under less pressure, sleep better, make sounder business decisions, give more time to my family, and am generally a much happier, and I hope, more useful member of society."

This man made his great spiritual discovery by *acting as if*.

The Next Step

After thirty years of teaching I never cease to wonder at some aspects of academic life. One of these is the wonderful sense of beginning again each semester. No matter what happened in the last semester we have another new opportunity to start again.

Then there is that great moment for every student, when having completed all his work he is graduated in a ceremony known as the commencement. It would seem that a more appropriate term would be "conclusion," but the word really means that having concluded academic work the student is now ready to go out into the real world and commence his life work. Which is what I am trying to say to you.

Are you convinced about the Decisive Motivational Action?

If you are still skeptical, perish the thought, it doesn't make too much difference. Involve yourself in an experiment. Accept the hypothesis that by utilizing the Decisive Motivational Action you can move into the fast lane of life, move from attitude to action, become positively addicted, add years to your life, overcome procrastination, unleash new creative potentialities, continue to steadily move ahead, gain immeasurably by giving, learn to control your emotions, discover new vistas of spiritual experience, acquire skills in using humor in your work, and a new way of attacking life's most difficult problems.

What have you got to lose?

Act as if and take a Decisive Motivational Action.

12
God Is a Verb

Faith is an exercise of the intellect, they say. It is further claimed that faith sometimes involves the emotion powers of personality, but seldom, if ever, the willing or volitional aspects of personality.

Well perhaps.

It is not difficult to produce some pretty convincing evidence to show that the will, the volitional part of personality, may play a much more important role in the development of faith than we have acknowledged in the past.

Action is an important ingredient of faith.

Preach Faith Until You Have Faith

John Wesley, the founder of Methodism, followed a tortuous pathway in his quest for faith. He had spent many hours following the pathway of mysticism without success. Then he met the Moravian, Peter Böhler.

Wesley asked him, "Do you think I should give up preaching until I have faith?"

Böhler replied, "No, keep on preaching faith until you get faith, and because you have faith you will preach faith."

Wesley took his advice and shortly afterwards had his "heart warming" experience which gave him the assurance, in his own words, "that I did trust in Christ and Christ alone for my salvation." His personal conversion propelled him into the great evangelical revival of the eighteenth century. Action was a vital factor in the experience and seems to have played a large part in clarifying Wesley's faith.

DECISIVE MOTIVATIONAL ACTION #12

Engage in a program of action that will have the effect of developing and deepening your spiritual life. Discover the way that the actionist can teach the mystic the secrets of vital Christian living accompanied by unanticipated material prosperity.

Walter Houston Clark, an authority in the field of psychology of religion, discussed the subject of religious conversion and noted the necessity for the concrete expression of the individual's faith. He quoted Wesley's experience and added, "Curiously enough, this stage [activity] may precede the crisis, when it doubtless plays an important part in bringing the crisis about."

Action can lead us into the most important of all human experiences in helping a man enter into a right relationship with God.

THE MOVEMENT OF THE BODY MAY PLAY AN IMPORTANT PART IN THE DEVELOPMENT OF THE SOUL

Following the stand of Martin Luther against the corruption of the medieval Catholic church, the Reformation movement took off and spread across Europe. For a period of time it must have looked to the reformers as if the whole of the continent was going to capitulate to the reformed faith. But the Catholic church was not about to surrender so easily.

The answer of Catholicism came in the form of a movement which historians called the Counter Reformation. The shock troops of this enterprise were the members of the Company of Jesus, a remarkable organization of zealots headed up by an unusual man, Ignatius Loyola.

A Soldier for God

The expression "shock troops" is appropriate. Loyola himself had been a soldier, and following a siege in which he was so badly injured that he could not go to battle again, he decided to become a soldier for God. To this day the leader of the Jesuit organization is referred to as the General. The training practices of the Society of Jesus were characterized by an intensity and thoroughness that would leave a marine boot camp standing still.

Each Jesuit was required to undertake the unique Spiritual Exercises. In devising them, Loyola drew heavily on his own personal experiences. During the time of his spiritual struggle and depression he noted the relationship between the movement of his body and his spiritual and emotional condition.

His Spiritual Exercises were full of directions concerning

actions to be taken while engaging in them. Some of the material for consideration had to be pondered while standing upright, some while walking to and fro in the priest's cell, some while sitting, others while kneeling, and yet others when stretched prone on the floor. Here again, action is a factor in the religious life of individuals.

AS ACTION MAY BE A FACTOR IN LEADING AN INDIVIDUAL TO AN EXPERIENCE OF FAITH AND THE DEVELOPMENT OF SPIRITUAL SKILLS; IT MAY ALSO BRING AN UNANTICIPATED MATERIAL BLESSING

Some thoughtful students of economics consider capitalism and the free enterprise system to be in part the offspring of a spirit of action produced by the motivations within Christianity. The Reformation may have spawned the idea. Previously, the organized church had looked upon work as punishment. Medieval Catholics read the story of the Garden of Eden and noted the sentence that fell upon a disobedient Adam and Eve: "In the sweat of thy face shalt thou eat bread...." Work was a penalty for sin, irksome but to be endured as a punishment for the offense.

A New Meaning for Vocation

In the thirteenth century the reformers concluded that the church was misguided in its view of human toil and the whole idea stood in need of drastic revision. They noted that in the church the word *vocation* had a special meaning. It was a call. This call was a summons for the individual to forsake the sinful world and retreat to a monastery or a convent and spend his or her days pleasing God by studying about and worshiping Him.

Luther, the ex-monk, was particularly trenchant in his criticism of this idea. He said, "There is no special religious vocation since the call of God comes to each man at the common task." "The lowlier the task, the better. The milkmaid and the carter of manure are doing a work more pleasing to God than the psalm-singing of the Carthusian." So was born the idea that an individual's work (actions) was his vocation or calling.

Max Weber's essay, *The Protestant Ethic and the Spirit of Capitalism*, drew many of its conclusions from the Reformation idea of vocation or calling, and the resulting attitude toward work. Weber saw two main elements in a new developing idea. The first was the Reformation concept of work as being a worthwhile activity in its own right to which a man had been called of God. The second, the Puritan conviction that personal indulgence was to be avoided.

The Three Rules of Christian Prudence

The twin concepts became an important part of the Protestant tradition and in Wesley's day he expressed it in a sermon titled "The Use of Money." Wesley took as his text one of the most enigmatic statements of Jesus: "I say unto you, make to yourselves friends of the mammon of unrighteousness; that, when ye fail, they may receive you into everlasting habitations" (Luke 16:9). He saw the text as a lesson to Christians about the way in which they should use money and deduced his noteworthy Three Rules of Christian Prudence.

Rule One: Gain All You Can

If a man's work is God's calling, then it should be very carefully chosen and entered upon. Wesley warned his followers to not become involved in employment that might damage others or might be a danger to their own health.

But having decided on their line of work, they were urged to really go into action with a series of exhortations. "Don't waste time spending idle moments on frivolous activities or being diverted from your work." He would also say, "Never leave anything undone; don't put it off." He concluded his exhortation with a stern warning: "Let nothing be done by halves, or in a light and careless manner. Let nothing in your business be left undone if it can be done by labor and patience."

Through exhortations like this, Christians came to see their work as the call of God and labored diligently to advance their businesses and jobs. Many of these early Methodists established their own businesses, which might have been a reason why the soldier Napoleon Bonaparte derisively referred to the English as "a nation of shopkeepers."

Earning money was seen to be honorable and highly desirable.

Rule Two: Save All You Can

While a highly-motivated, industrious spirit undoubtedly brought more rewards as people paid heed to Wesley's exhortation, "earn all you can," another factor entered to multiply the products of such industry. These hardworking people had entered upon a way of life that called for self-denial.

Wesley was concerned lest the rewards of industry should be lost. So he warned his followers about indulging themselves with expensive foods which he saw as "a respectable kind of sensuality," and "elegant epicureanism." He urged his followers to "cut off all this expense! Despise delicacy and variety, and be content with what plain nature requires."

IT IS NOT SO MUCH THE AMOUNT YOU EARN AS HOW MUCH OF YOUR EARNINGS YOU RETAIN

From food he moved to warn about extravagance in dress, warning against, "superfluous or expensive apparel or needless ornaments."

Then he took up the matter of housing, reminding them of the way they could waste their money, "in superfluous or expensive furniture, in costly furnishings, gilding, books; in elegant rather than useful gardens."

This keen student of human nature was also aware of the subtle temptation that beset parents in their concern for their children. He warned about spending too much money on children and lamented, "How amazing then is the infatuation of those parents who think they can never leave their children enough," and warned parents against such an attitude.

Be thrifty and frugal, was Wesley's message.

Rule Three: Give All You Can

The third rule was the logical extension of this wise man's theorizing. He was well aware of the dangers that would beset his followers as they followed rules one and two. Following these gave rise to an interesting paradigm of which Weber was aware when he wrote his essay.

HARD WORK + FRUGALITY = ACCUMULATION

Wesley feared that his two first laws might be too successful. He feared that the accumulation of money would cause his people to become indolent, to sit back and enjoy their wealth and lose their fervor. So he added the third maxim: "Give all you can."

The plan of action became:

Earn all you can
Save all you can
Give all you can

The third law gave Wesley the opportunity to discuss the all-important matter of stewardship. He showed that God is the Possessor of all, who has placed the believer as a steward rather than a possessor. Christians must consider all they have as a sacred trust from God and realize that they must dispose of portions of these possessions to the family of God from time to time.

It is easier for a camel to go through the eye of a needle, than for a rich man to enter into the kingdom of God.

Jesus

Wesley's idea had a certain touch of genius about it. At the heart of it all was action, hard work at one's job, living a frugal life, and acquiring a means of distributing to the whole household of faith.

Of course, the natural outcome of distribution was to go to work once again and give oneself to the earning of more money. It was a certain pathway to action.

Mysticism and Movement

It seems very natural to assert that the great leaders and personalities of the religious world have been contemplative men, men who withdrew from the hubbub of civilization's maddening crowd and found some isolated spot where they could listen for the voice of God. That is true except for those who were feverishly rushing toward people, living long and crowded days with little rest and time for contemplation. Such men were John Wesley and a host of others who have played important roles in the history of the church.

The mystic and the actionist have each played significant parts and it may be that in glorifying the mystic we have overlooked the importance of the actionist.

Jesus reserved his wrath for the most heinous sins of men and women. He seldom spoke in this vein, but when He did He declared in no uncertain terms. His condemnation of one man was that he should be cast into outer darkness, a horrible place where "there shall be weeping and gnashing of teeth" (Matthew 22:13).

What was this man's offense? Adultery? Murder? Hypocrisy? Lying? Stealing? No, none of these. He did nothing—absolutely nothing—and because he did nothing he was condemned.

For he that hath, to him shall be given; and he that hath not, from him shall be taken even that which he hath.

Jesus

The Savior was on the side of the actionists. He laid down the principle that activity and use enhances the original gifts—while failure to use one's ability means deterioration and ultimately decay. Use it or lose it.

Leisure and I have taken leave of one another.

Wesley

Wesley becomes the illustration of the action principle. He wrote or edited 233 books including volumes on history, logic, medicine, Greek and French grammar, and made a notable resolution, "Leisure and I have taken leave of one another. I propose to be busy as long as I live."

He lived up to his resolution. Sometimes called the Happy Traveler, in a forty-year period he traveled, mainly on horseback, a quarter of a million miles, crossed the Irish Channel fifty times, averaged twenty miles a day and preached forty thousand sermons. His journal contains many references to his full days as "hurry days." Small wonder Wesley moved a nation closer to God. He was an actionist for his Lord.

Is God a Verb?

Is God really a verb? The Spanish translations of the New Testament certainly say so. Where our English translation says, "In the beginning was the *Word*...." some Spanish translations say *Verbo*.

All the evidence goes to show that God is a Verb. He is active, first in creating, then in redeeming, and now in sustaining. It is not unreasonable to believe that His followers who are people of faith should also be actionists. The New Testament reaffirms this theme especially in the Epistle to the Hebrews which gives us a definition of faith and proceeds to tell of the exploits of people who had faith.

Who, through faith, subdued kingdoms,
wrought righteousness,
obtained promises,
stopped the mouths of lions,
quenched the violence of fire,
escaped the edge of the sword,

out of weakness were made strong,
waxed valiant in fight. . . .
                    Hebrews 11:33, 34

These actionists are worthy followers of the God who is a Verb!

The Family Perspective

The single most important institution for teaching Christianity is the home, and in the home the family altar is the significant instrument in that task.

We have already mentioned the family meal as a setting for teaching and for family fun. But by far the family altar is the most potent element, for it becomes the spiritual center of the family. The two—the family meal and the altar—are usually experienced together. The altar not only strengthens the relationship of family members to God; one study shows that a significant difference can be observed in the relationships within the family where the altar is maintained regularly.

What do we need to have a successful family altar?

1. A clear recognition of the place of family rituals by commencing the meal with a blessing offered by a family member.

2. A time of sharing at the evening meal, as family members recount experiences of the day, difficulties or triumphs encountered.

3. A season of prayer in which family members and friends are prayed for.

4. An experience of reading the Scriptures by one or more of the family members.

5. All of the above completed in a short period of time so that the children will not be aversively conditioned.

One of Robert Burns's beautiful poems is called the "The Cotter's Saturday Night." The cotter was a peasant farmer and Saturday night was significant because all the week's work was done and the Sabbath on the morrow would be a day of rest.

The cheerfu' supper done, wi' serious face,
they, round the ingle, form a circle wide;
The sire turns o'er wi' patriarchal grace,
The big ha' Bible, ance his father's pride.
His bonnet reverently is laid aside,
His [grey hair's] wearing thin and bare;
Those strains that once did sweet in Zion glide,
He wales a portion with judicious care,
And, "Let us worship God!" he says, with solemn air....

The priest-like father reads the sacred page....

Then kneeling down to Heaven's Eternal King,
The saint, the father, and the husband prays....

In this act of worship, not only is the family unit strengthened but surely the heart of God must be pleased.

THE FAMILY THAT PRAYS TOGETHER STAYS TOGETHER

Epilogue

 Do you still have a lingering doubt about the validity of the Decisive Motivational Action?

Think again about its potentialities.

Consider a man who through losing his own vision was able to give sight to generations of other people. William Hickling Prescott enrolled in Harvard University to study law. While sitting at the meal table, a fellow student threw a hard crust of bread which struck Prescott in the eye and ultimately caused him to lose his sight.

After graduation, Prescott went to work in his father's law office, but realized that a career in law was not a practical possibility. He took a series of Decisive Motivational Actions.

- He decided to enter the field of literary research.
- He procured a device called a noctograph from England. It consisted of a frame with brass wires along which he could write without the lines running together.
- Having to depend on others to read to him, he perfected a

185

memorization technique and became so proficient at memorizing that he was able to hold sixty pages of printed material—about three times the capacity of at least one very popular lap computer—in his memory.
- He developed a method of creative thinking by which he was able to turn this material over in his mind as he walked or was driven.

Losing his own sight, Prescott gave eyes to others. He had never seen Mexico and Peru, but he *acted as if* he had his eyesight and researched the history of these countries so carefully that he was able to write about and describe them with great skill in his *History of the Conquest of Mexico and Peru*. His writings were done with such a flair that sighted people who read his books felt they had an intimate knowledge of these countries through Prescott's beautifully-written works.

HUMAN BEINGS HAVE THE CAPACITY TO TURN A MINUS INTO A PLUS

Your first step will be a Decisive Motivational Action.

Notes

1. Charles Dickens, *Nicholas Nickleby* (New York: Penguin Books, 1978), 82.
2. Ibid., 95.
3. Ibid., 150.
4. Laurence Cherry, "On the Real Benefits of Eustress," *Psychology Today* (March 1978), 60.
5. William Glasser, *Positive Addiction* (New York: Harper & Row, 1976), 93.
6. David A. Fryxell, "Outfiguring the Navy" (*American Way*, May 1984), 39–42.
7. Daniel J. Leithauser, *Early Ambulation and Related Procedures in Surgical Management* (Springfield: Charles C. Thomas, 1946), 146.
8. Carol J. Bellis, "Immediate Unrestricted Activity after Operation" (*International Surgery*, April 1971).
9. Kenneth H. Cooper, *The Aerobics Program for Total Well-Being* (New York: M. Evans and Company, 1982), 12.
10. Larry Wood, "Landry: The Supreme Commander" (*American Way*, September 1983), 76.